# Underestimated

## Second Edition

# Underestimated:

## Our Not So Peaceful Nuclear Future

By

Henry D. Sokolski

Nonproliferation Policy Education Center

Copyright © 2017 by Henry D. Sokolski
Nonproliferation Policy Education Center
Arlington, VA 22209
www.npolicy.org

2017
Printed in the United States of America

All rights reserved. Except for brief quotations in a review, this book, or parts thereof, must not be reproduced in any form without permission in writing from the Nonproliferation Policy Education Center.

ISBN 978-0-9862895-5-2

Cover design by Amanda Sokolski

*To Victor Gilinsky,
a mentor and a friend*

# Contents

*List of Figures* ii
*Preface* iii
*Foreword* by Andrew W. Marshall iv
*Acknowledgements* vi
*List of Acronyms* ix

Introduction 1

**Chapter 1: What We Think** 6

**Chapter 2: Where We Are Headed** 44

**Chapter 3: What Might Help** 97

Index 125

# List of Figures

**Figure 1:** Nuclear Proliferation: What We Think

**Figure 2:** From U.S. Strategic Dominance to a Compressed Nuclear Crowd

**Figure 3:** National Stockpiles of Separated Plutonium

**Figure 4:** National Stockpiles of Highly-Enriched Uranium

**Figure 5:** Four Nuclear Weapons States in 1962

**Figure 6:** How the U.S. Views the World Today

**Figure 7:** Possible Proliferated Future

**Figure 8:** Russian Underground Nuclear Complex at Yamantau

**Figure 9:** China's Underground Great Wall

**Figure 10:** Nuclear-Capable Missile Countries Today

**Figure 11:** The Next Decade: Nuclear Weapons Uncertainties

**Figure 12:** Japanese Plutonium Stocks and Projected Production

**Figure 13:** Current and Projected East Asian Uranium Enrichment Capacities

**Figure 14:** States Planning to Have Their First Nuclear Power Reactor by or before 2035

# Preface

It has been nearly three years since the release of the first edition of *Underestimated: Our Not So Peaceful Nuclear Future*. Since then, North Korea has conducted two nuclear tests, the United States agreed to a multilateral nuclear deal limiting Iran's nuclear program, and we have a new president who is eager to question all aspects of U.S. policy, including those related to national security and nuclear policy. Other important nuclear developments have occurred as well. These are all reflected in the edits that have been made to this second edition.

My original decision to keep this publication open source was sound. All of the book's footnotes have URLs for the references, which in the electronic version of the book (available at *http://www.npolicy.org/thebook.php?bid=34*) can be accessed merely by clicking on them. In addition, hard copies of the second edition can be bought for a discounted price at Amazon.com. The aim of this book is not to make money, but to focus and provoke discussion about how we should think and act against further spread of nuclear weapons and their possible use. Work has already begun on the third edition.

*Henry D. Sokolski*

# Foreword

Henry Sokolski has written an excellent, short book about what he sees as our not so peaceful nuclear future. While short in length, it covers a lot of ground, and because it is extensively footnoted, it can lead readers to the broader literature.

The book provides a good picture of the growing stockpiles of separated plutonium and the stockpiles of highly-enriched uranium, as well as the likely expansion of nuclear power programs in additional countries. When reading the book, my thoughts turned to the Per Bak book, *How Nature Works*, and the concept of self-organized criticality and its descriptions of computer simulations and experiments leading to avalanches in sand piles. This may be a useful way of thinking about the possible consequences for nuclear weapon proliferation as the stockpiles of fissile material grow.

Also, as we think about the likelihood of the proliferation of nuclear weapons, we should be aware that developing nuclear weapons may be easier as time passes and computing power increases, high energy explosives improve, and diagnostic technology advances.

Sokolski includes a discussion of the question, does it matter if more countries have nuclear weapons. He points out that a number of respected people say it doesn't; some say it would be a more stable world. Sokolski disagrees; I am with him, for two reasons. First, those who say it won't matter, I believe, tend to assume that deterrence of attacks by others is almost automatic. There is little discussion of the vulnerability of the weapons, delivery systems, command and central systems, and more. Having a well-protected second-strike capability historically was not automatic; it took time and effort, changed operational practices, etc. Second, the Russians have been writing for at least the past fifteen years of the need they have for tactical nuclear weapons to defend their large territory, because they say they do not have the resources to defend conventionally. They call for a new generation of nuclear weapons that would be easier to use. They more recently have developed an interest in the early use of tactical nuclear weapons to quickly de-escalate a conflict.

If such use occurred, especially if it led to the successful de-escalation of a conflict on their borders, it might be a trigger for an avalanche of proliferation, a la Per Bak's sand piles, a much larger avalanche than, in the case of Iran, getting nuclear weapons, which has been the subject of several studies in recent years. The successful Russian use would be the first operational use of nuclear weapons in many decades and would revive consideration of the value of tactical nuclear weapons. In any case, it is not clear that this would be a very peaceful world.

The problems arising from the growing stockpiles are addressed in the book and some ideas are put forward—a good start on how to limit the dangers that may flow from that growth. The author raises important questions that deserve continued attention.

*Andrew W. Marshall*

# Acknowledgements

When I first set out to write this book in fulfillment of an overly ambitious proposal I made years ago (and that, to my astonishment, got fully funded), I had something much longer in mind. After having published various bits of this original project elsewhere,[1] though, I became convinced that with

---

1. See Henry Sokolski, "Taking Proliferation Seriously," *Policy Review*, October and November 2003, available from *http://www.npolicy.org/article_file/Taking_Proliferation_Seriously-Policy_Review.pdf*; "Too Speculative: Getting Serious About Nuclear Terrorism," *The New Atlantis*, Fall 2006, available from *http://www.npolicy.org/article_file/Too_Speculative-Getting_Serious_About_Nuclear_Terrorism.pdf*; *Falling Behind: International Scrutiny of the Peaceful Atom*, Carlisle, PA: Strategic Studies Institute, March 2008, pp. 3-61, available from *http://npolicy.org/thebook.php?bid=5#intro*; "Avoiding a Nuclear Crowd: How to Resist the Weapon's Spread," *Policy Review*, June 1, 2009, available from *http://www.hoover.org/research/avoiding-nuclear-crowd*; Henry Sokolski and Victor Gilinsky, "Locking down the NPT," *Bulletin of the Atomic Scientists*, June 17, 2009, available from *http://www.npolicy.org/article_file/Locking_down_the_NPT.pdf*; "The High and Hidden Costs of Nuclear Power," *Policy Review*, August 1, 2010, available from *http://www.hoover.org/research/high-and-hidden-costs-nuclear-power*; "Missiles for Peace," *Armed Forces Journal*, August 1, 2010, available from *http://www.armedforcesjournal.com/missiles-for-peace/*; *Controlling the Further Spread of Nuclear Weapons*, New York: The Council on Foreign Relations, April 26, 2010, available from *http://npolicy.org/article.php?aid=134&rt=&key=council on foreign relations&sec=article&author=*; "The Untapped Potential of the NPT," *The New Atlantis*, November 1, 2010, available from *http://www.thenewatlantis.com/publications/the-untapped-potential-of-the-npt*; "The Post Fukushima Arms Race," *Foreign Policy*,

such a complex topic, brevity was the best way to reach busy professionals.[2] Hence, this short volume. Its aim, to spotlight the potential dark spots in our nuclear future, is less academic than it is practical.

Among those who lent material and moral support were my key funders and my wife, Amanda, who designed the book's cover. They humored me well beyond any reasonable requirement of civility. My staff at the Nonproliferation Policy Education Center also deserve acknowledgement, particularly my research assistant, Kate Harrison, whose reminders and research support were all too necessary and Leon Whyte, who provided essential support for completion of this second edition. I also would like to thank John Mearsheimer of the University of Chicago, who kindly invited me to present the first of this book's three chapters before the University's Program on International Security Policy workshop series.

The University of Utah's Hinckley Institute of Politics and the Tanner Center for Human Rights; The Institute of World Politics, where I teach; The University of San Diego and the University of California at San Diego; Arizona State University; Sandia, Lawrence Livermore, and Los Alamos National Laboratories; The Naval Postgraduate School; Colorado State University; and the Carnegie Endowment in Washington, D.C. were also kind enough

---

July 29, 2011, available from *http://foreignpolicy.com/2011/07/30/the-post-fukushima-arms-race/*; "Ten Regrets: America's Nonproliferation Efforts Against Iran," in Joachim Krause, ed., *Iran's Nuclear Program,* London: Routledge, 2012, pp. 69-83, available from *http://npolicy.org/article_file/Ten_Regrets-Americas_Nonproliferation_Efforts_against_Iran.pdf*; and "Serious Rules for Nuclear Power without Proliferation," *The Nonproliferation Review,* February 18, 2014, pp. 77-98, available from *http://www.npolicy.org/article.php?aid=1203&rt=&key=serious%20rules&sec=article&author=*.

2. See Mary Keeley, "Word Confusion," *Books and Such* (blog), February 27, 2014, available from *http://www.booksandsuch.com/blog/word-count-confusion/*.

to host my presentation of earlier versions of the materials finalized in this volume.

Additional support for this volume came from several individuals over a much longer period. These include Thomas Blau, Fred Iklé, James Lilley, Andrew Marshall, Harry Rowen, and Marin Strmecki. Finally, Victor Gilinsky, who I have had the privilege of knowing for more than 35 years, has made everything I have pursued in the field of nuclear policy far more interesting than it would be otherwise. I'd like to think that if I have gotten anything right in this book, it's his fault.

# List of Acronyms

| | |
|---|---|
| **ANZUS** | Australia, New Zealand, United States Security Treaty |
| **CTBT** | Comprehensive Nuclear-Test-Ban Treaty |
| **DF** | Dongfeng, Chinese for "East Wind," designation for ballistic missiles |
| **FBR** | fast breeder reactor |
| **FMCT** | Fissile Material Cut-off Treaty |
| **HEU** | highly-enriched uranium |
| **IAEA** | International Atomic Energy Agency |
| **ICBM** | intercontinental ballistic missile |
| **INF** | Intermediate-Range Nuclear Forces Treaty |
| **MIRV** | multiple independently targetable re-entry vehicles |
| **MOX** | mixed oxide fuel |
| **MTCR** | Missile Technology Control Regime |
| **NPT** | Nuclear Nonproliferation Treaty |
| **SLBM** | submarine-launched ballistic missile |
| **START** | Strategic Arms Reductions Treaty |
| **UAE** | United Arab Emirates |
| **WMD** | Weapons of Mass Destruction |

# INTRODUCTION

It was curious and sad that after his death, Albert Wohlstetter, a former professor of mine and a major force in American strategic planning for nearly a half century, was criticized for not having written a book. His apologia, albeit unspoken, was that he had more important things to do guiding U.S. and international policy, which he did effectively in so many ways, including framing the debate over what should be done about nuclear proliferation. His work, and that of his wife and chief collaborator, Roberta Wohlstetter, are best understood through the many policy and economic studies they wrote and the profound impact they had on U.S. and allied security and energy policies.[3]

Although I served 11 years in the Pentagon and as a staffer on Capitol Hill, I have no such excuse. The clearest proof of this is this slim volume, the sequel to *Best of Intentions: America's Campaign Against Strategic Weapons Proliferation*.[4] That volume was largely historical and written in support of a graduate-level course I teach on nuclear energy policy. The thinking behind *Best of Inten-*

---

3. See Robert Zarate and Henry Sokolski, ed., *Nuclear Heuristics: Selected Writings of Albert and Roberta Wohlstetter,* Carlisle, PA: Strategic Studies Institute, 2009.

4. See Henry D. Sokolski, *Best of Intentions: America's Campaign against Strategic Weapons Proliferation,* Westport, CT: Praeger, 2001.

*tions* was straightforward: Determining where we are necessarily requires familiarity first with where we have been. I wrote that volume because, at the time, there was no critical history of nonproliferation available to dispatch my students in any practical direction.

As I continued to teach, though, I noticed another gap in the literature. The arguments policymakers and academics were making on how nuclear weapons reductions related to preventing further nuclear proliferation were, at best, uneven. Each of the basic views—arms control, hawkish, and academic—spotlighted some important aspect of the truth, but each was incomplete and surprisingly optimistic.

The view most arms control proponents propound is that any state that has nuclear weapons is obliged to make further nuclear weapons reductions under the Nuclear Nonproliferation Treaty (NPT). The superpowers promised to make such reductions, they contend, to get nonweapons states to accept intrusive nuclear inspections and to abstain from acquiring nuclear arms. Most who hold this view also believe that nuclear weapons are only useful to deter others' use of these weapons, that this mission can be accomplished with relatively few nuclear weapons, and that, as such, we can make significant, additional strategic arms reductions at little or no cost to our national security. Pursuing such reductions and strengthening existing nuclear security measures also are desirable, they argue, because nuclear weapons and their related production infrastructures are vulnerable to unauthorized or accidental firings, terrorist seizure, sabotage, and possible use.

Almost all of those holding these views argue that states with advanced "peaceful" nuclear technology are obliged to share it with nonweapons states as a quid pro quo to get these states to uphold their NPT nonproliferation pledges. Thus, civilian nuclear sharing, nonproliferation, and strategic arms reductions are viewed as three equally critical "pillars" of an NPT "bargain."[5]

A second, more hawkish view rejects these positions, arguing that the link between nuclear reductions and proliferation is negative: Further significant nuclear weapons cuts could well encourage America's adversaries to "sprint to nuclear parity."[6] Such efforts, in turn, could easily spook Washington's allies who lack nuclear weapons (e.g., Turkey, Saudi Arabia, South Korea, and Japan) to hedge their security bets by acquiring their own. To avoid such proliferation, this group contends that keeping or increasing U.S. nuclear weapons capabilities (especially vis-à-vis China and Russia) is our best bet.

Finally, some academics are skeptical of both of these views. They identify themselves as "neorealists." They are divided roughly into two camps—those who believe that nuclear deterrence works and those that do not. Their disagreement here is significant but not as great as what unifies their thinking—a shared disbelief in there being any major link between nuclear weapons reductions, nonproliferation, and international security.

Mainstream neorealists emphasize what they believe to be the au-

---

5. See U.S. Department of State, U.S. Delegation to the 2010 Nuclear Nonproliferation Treaty Review Conference, *Treaty on the Non-Proliferation of Nuclear Weapons*, "The Three Pillars," pp. 4-6, available from *http://www.state.gov/documents/organization/141503.pdf*; Paul Kerr, et. al., *The 2010 Nonproliferation Treaty (NPT) Review Conference: Key Issues and Implications*, RL41216, Washington DC: U.S. Congressional Research Service, May 3, 2010, pp. 1-15, available from *http://fas.org:8080/sgp/crs/nuke/R41216.pdf*; and Wikipedia, *Treaty on the Non-Proliferation of Nuclear Weapons*, last modified October 6, 2014, available from *http://en.wikipedia.org/wiki/Treaty_on_the_Non-Proliferation_of_Nuclear_Weapons#Treaty_.22pillars.22*.

6. See National Security Implications of the Strategic Offensive Reductions Treaty: Senate Hearing 107-806, Before the U.S. Senate Committee on the Armed Forces, 107th Cong. (July 25, 2002) (statement of Donald H. Rumsfeld, Secretary of Defense), available from *http://www.globalsecurity.org/military/library/congress/2002_hr/rumsfeld725.pdf*.

tomaticity of nuclear deterrence. They contend that the further spread of nuclear weapons is far less harmful to the world's security than is commonly assumed and that, because nuclear weapons are so effective in deterring wars, their further proliferation could actually help keep the peace.

A second and more recent neorealist school, though, rejects faith in nuclear deterrence. It sees little military value in nuclear weapons but (for this reason) also concludes that their further spread is largely inconsequential. As for trying to prevent proliferation, this newer school of neorealism argues this can be far more dangerous and provocative—they spotlight the invasion of Iraq—than letting these weapons spread.[7]

Each of these views—arms control, hawkish, and academic—is intellectually attractive. Each is concise. All, however, are incomplete. None fully explore the regional insecurities that arise with threatened nuclear weapons breakouts or ramp-ups. Instead, they dwell on the security impacts of nuclear proliferation after states have actually broken out or ramped up. Nor do they have much to say about the significant overlaps between civilian and military nuclear activities or the risk that "peaceful" nuclear facilities or materials might be diverted to make bombs. Instead, they focus almost exclusively on nuclear weapons and their impact on international

---

7. The best single work reflecting the views of the first camp is Kenneth N. Waltz's essay in Scott D. Sagan and Kenneth N. Waltz, *The Spread of Nuclear Weapons: A Debate,* New York: W.W. Norton & Company, 1995. The best work reflecting the views of the second camp is John Mueller, *Atomic Obsession: Nuclear Alarmism from Hiroshima to Al-Qaeda,* New York: Oxford University Press, 2010. As for the arguments made about the human costs of war against Iraq, there is no question that these were substantial. That the war was fought primarily as a nonproliferation campaign, however, is much more open to debate. See, e.g., Jamie McIntyre, "Pentagon Challenges *Vanity Fair* Report," *CNN,* May 30, 2003, available from *http://www.cnn.com/2003/US/05/30/wolfowitz. vanity.fair/.*

security (albeit in differing time frames).[8] Finally, none adequately considers the discontiguous view that fewer nuclear weapons in fewer hands is desirable but that rushing to achieve such reductions without first getting key nuclear states to reduce in a transparent, coordinated fashion could easily make matters worse.

This brief volume covers each of these points. First, it reviews the key popular views on nuclear proliferation. Second, it considers how much worse matters might get if states continue with relatively loose nuclear constraints on civilian and military nuclear activities. Finally, it suggests what might be done to avoid the worst.

---

8. The first school—the official arms control view—is both incremental and relatively immediate in its outlook, activities, goals, and approach. It generally views reaching any agreement, even an interim one, as being favorable to reaching no agreement. In contrast, hawkish supporters of nuclear weapons (as well as hard-headed security planners who might not be as enthusiastic about relying heavily on nuclear arms) generally focus on set goals and encourage actions for the mid-term—i.e., for the next 10 to 20 years. Finally, academic skeptics who challenge these other schools generally write as if their operational insights about nuclear weapons and deterrence immediately pertain and are permanent, i.e., immutable.

# WHAT WE THINK

For the last half century, the task of limiting nuclear arsenals has been viewed as being related to but different from preventing proliferation. Nuclear arms restraints are "fostered" through nuclear weapons negotiations, agreements, and norms as well as by states deploying "stable" strategic weapons forces—i.e., ones that can readily survive even if they are struck first and that are themselves incapable of totally destroying a key opponent's nuclear forces in a first strike. In contrast, one "fights" or "combats" the further spread of nuclear weapons by imposing export controls, economic sanctions, international inspections, or conducting preventative and preemptive military strikes and covert intelligence and military operations.[9] The most significant nuclear arms control efforts historically have been undertaken by the most heavily nuclear-armed states—principally the United States and Russia. Preventing nuclear proliferation, in contrast, is generally a global undertaking.

The Obama administration is noteworthy among recent presidencies for consciously trying to integrate U.S. nuclear arms control efforts with nonproliferation. Following President Barack Obama's 2009

---

9. Sometime, roughly in the early 1990s, it became fashionable to talk about "combating" proliferation. A Google search of "combating proliferation" as of June 7, 2016, yielded 475,000 results.

appeal to eliminate nuclear weapons presented in Prague,[10] the U.S. government made reducing nuclear arms a prerequisite for preventing their further spread. If we expect other nations to repress their own nuclear weapons aspirations, administration officials argued, the nuclear superpowers had to demonstrate a greater willingness to disarm themselves. Such disarmament was feasible, they insisted, because nuclear weapons were, in their view, only useful to deter other hostile nuclear weapons states. This basic mission, they argued, could be accomplished with a relatively small stockpile of nuclear weapons. On the other hand, maintaining large stockpiles of nuclear weapons and nuclear weapons-usable fuels, they argued, only increased the prospects for instability, nuclear terrorism, and accidental or illicit use.

Hawkish supporters of nuclear weapons have a different view.[11] They argue that reducing American and Russian nuclear arms has little or no impact on reducing others' nuclear weapons activities or holdings (e.g., North Korea and Iran). Instead, reducing America's nuclear arsenal might only entice China to build up to America's current nuclear numbers and encourage America's key nonnuclear allies and friends—e.g., South Korea, Japan, Saudi Arabia, and Turkey—to hedge their bets against decreasingly credible U.S. nuclear security guarantees by developing nuclear weapons options

---

10. See "Remarks by President Barack Obama," Hradcany Square, Prague, Czech Republic, April 5, 2009, available from *iipdigital.usembassy.gov/st/english/texttrans/2009/04/20090406115740eaifas0.9701763.html#axzz4XetYocFS*.

11. The term "hawk" and "hawkish" in this book is used as shorthand for hawkish supporters of nuclear weapons. This is a concession to popular usage. It is hardly concise. The first use of the term "hawk" was made during the War of 1812. It referred to those who saw war as being the solution to America's troubles with the United Kingdom. Today, however, there are many that support America's maintenance of its nuclear arsenal who are anything but eager to go to war. There also are many security advocates and experts that may be willing to go to war in many cases but who hardly favor relying heavily on nuclear weapons for U.S. security.

of their own. Finally, they argue, nuclear weapons, especially in U.S. and allied hands, have helped keep the peace, whereas letting U.S. and allied nuclear arsenals decline quantitatively or qualitatively only increases the prospects for war.[12]

A group of academic skeptics, who identify themselves as neorealists, also question if eliminating nuclear weapons is critical to assure peace. Further nuclear weapons proliferation may be inevitable they argue, but it's unlikely to be destabilizing. A credible nuclear deterrent force that holds several major cities at risk, they insist, can keep the peace and need only be a relatively small, "finite" force. The earliest proponents of such "finite deterrence"—Pierre Gallois, his French colleagues,[13] Admiral Arleigh A. Burke, and other original supporters of the U.S. Polaris nuclear missile submarine fleet[14] and, much later, Kenneth Waltz and his academic asso-

---

12. See, e.g., Loren Thompson, "Nuclear Weapons: How Few Is Too Few," *Forbes,* May 28, 2013, available from *http://www.forbes.com/sites/lorenthompson/2013/05/28/nuclear-weapons-cuts-how-few-is-too-few/*; Congressman Doug Lamborn, "Six Reasons Obama's Plan to Give Up Our Nukes Is a Really Bad Idea," *The Heritage Foundry* (blog), June 20, 2013, available from *http://dailysignal.com/2013/06/20/guest-post-6-reasons-obamas-plan-to-give-up-our-nukes-is-a-really-bad-idea/*; and Robert Zarate, "Is Obama Pushing Unilateral Nuclear Cuts," *Time*, February 12, 2013, available from *http://nation.time.com/2013/02/12/is-obama-pushing-unilateral-nuclear-cuts/*.

13. See Pierre-Marie Gallois, *Stratégie de l'âge nucléaire,* Paris: Francois-Xavier de Guibert, 1960; Bruno Tertrais, "'Destruction Assurée': The Origins and Development of French Nuclear Strategy," in *Getting MAD: Nuclear Mutual Assured Destruction, Its Origins and Practice*, ed. Henry Sokolski, Carlisle, PA: Strategic Studies Institute, 2004, pp. 51-122, available from *npolicy.org/books/Getting_MAD/Ch2_Tertrais.pdf*; and David S. Yost, "France's Nuclear Deterrence Strategy: Concepts and Operations Implementation," in *Getting MAD*, pp. 197-237, available from *npolicy.org/books/Getting_MAD/Ch7_Yost.pdf*.

14. See Commander P. H. Backus, "Finite Deterrence, Controlled Retaliation," *U.S. Naval Institute Proceedings* 85, No. 3, March 1959, pp. 23-29; David Alan Rosenberg, "The Origins of Overkill: Nuclear Weapons and American Strategy 1945-1960," *International Security* 7, no. 4, Spring 1983, pp. 3-71; William Burr, "'How Much is Enough?': The U.S. Navy and 'Finite Deterrence,'" *National*

ciates[15]—all emphasized what they saw as the virtual automaticity of nuclear deterrence between any two rival nuclear-armed states. With this, French proponents of finite deterrence argued that the further proliferation of nuclear weapons to smaller states was more likely to prevent military aggression than to prompt it. Central to their thinking was the disturbing notion that credibly threatening to destroy an adversary's major cities (what Charles de Gaulle referred to as "tearing off an arm"[16]) would deter hostile actions by other states both large and small.

A more recent version of such thinking has been made popular by scholars such as John Mueller. Mueller takes a different tack but reaches similar conclusions. He argues that nuclear weapons actually do a poor job of deterring small or major wars.[17] Citing the popular scholarship of Ward Wilson,[18] supporters of this view

---

*Security Archive*, Electronic Briefing Book, no. 275, May 1, 2009, available from *http://www.gwu.edu/~nsarchiv/nukevault/ebb275/index.htm*; and Oskar Morgenstern, "The Oceanic System: The Invulnerable Force," in *The Question of National Defense,* New York: Random House, 1959.

15. See Kenneth N. Waltz, "Nuclear Myths and Political Realities," *American Political Science Review* 84, no. 3, September 1990, pp. 731-745; John J. Mearsheimer, "The Case for a Ukrainian Nuclear Deterrent," *Foreign Affairs* 72, no. 3, Summer 1993, pp. 50-80, available from *http://mearsheimer.uchicago.edu/pdfs/A0020.pdf*; Andrew Mack, "North Korea and the Bomb," *Foreign Policy* 83, Summer 1991, pp. 87-104; Michael D. Intriligator and Dagobert L. Brito, "Nuclear Proliferation and the Probability of Nuclear War," *Public Choice* 37, no. 2, 1981, pp. 247-259; and Bruce Bueno de Mesquita and William H. Riker, "An Assessment of the Merits of Selective Nuclear Proliferation," *Journal of Conflict Resolution* 26, no. 2, 1982, pp. 283-306.

16. See Pierre-Marie Gallois, "La dissuasion du faible au fort," in *L'aventure de la bombe: de Gaulle et la dissuasion nucléaire (1958-1969),* Paris: Plon, 1985, p. 170.

17. See Mueller, *Atomic Obsession.*

18. See Ward Wilson, "The Winning Weapon? Rethinking Nuclear Weapons in Light of Hiroshima," *International Security* 31, no. 4, Spring 2007, pp. 162-

contend that nuclear weapons were unnecessary to secure Japan's surrender in 1945[19] or to deter World War III since North Atlantic Treaty Organization (NATO) and Warsaw Pact nations were haunted by fears of suffering a yet deadlier conventionally-armed version of World War II (WWII).[20] Also, smaller wars—e.g., the Israeli War of '73 and the Korean and Vietnam wars—Mueller notes, clearly were not deterred by anyone's nuclear weapons. Nor were the terrorist attacks of 9/11 in 2001 or the terrorist attacks on Mumbai in 2008. The implication is that nuclear weapons are so ineffective at deterring aggression and their use is so unlikely that their further spread is not all that consequential.[21]

---

179, available from *http://belfercenter.ksg.harvard.edu/files/is3104_pp162-179_wilson.pdf*; "The Myth of Nuclear Deterrence," *Nonproliferation Review* 15, no. 3, November 2008, pp. 421-439, available from *http://cns.miis.edu/npr/pdfs/153_wilson.pdf*; and "The Bomb that Didn't Beat Japan...Stalin Did," *Foreign Policy*, May 30, 2013, available from *http://www.foreignpolicy.com/articles/2013/05/29/the_bomb_didnt_beat_japan_nuclear_world_war_ii*.

19. Such revisionist views about the nuclear bombing of Japan, which now find favor with liberal opponents of nuclear weapons, are oddly adaptations of arguments made from 1945 through the 1960s by some of the most hawkish and conservative of Americans. See Barton J. Bernstein, "American Conservatives Are the Forgotten Critics of the Atomic Bombings of Japan," *San Jose Mercury News,* August 2, 2014, available from *http://www.mercurynews.com/opinion/ci_26253535/barton-j-bernstein-american-conservatives-are-forgotten-critics*.

20. See John Mueller, "The Essential Irrelevance of Nuclear Weapons: Stability in the Postwar World," in *The Cold War and After: Prospects for Peace,* Cambridge, MA: MIT Press, 1997, pp. 45–69, available from *politicalscience.osu.edu/faculty/jmueller/ISESSIRR.PDF* and *Atomic Obsession,* pp. 29-48.

21. There, are, of course, more moderate views among those that might be pushed into this camp. This includes several prominent academics, such as Stephen M. Walt and Robert Jervis, who have challenged the assumed high value of nuclear weapons in deterring attacks but do not believe their value is necessarily zero and, therefore, are not entirely comfortable with their further proliferation. See e.g., Stephen M. Walt, "Rethinking the 'Nuclear Revolution'" *NPR*, July 6, 2014, available from *http://www.publicbroadcasting.net/kbia/.artsmain/article/1/1338/1684234/Columns/Foreign.Policy.Rethinking.The.'Nuclear. Revolution* and Robert Jervis, "Why Nuclear Superiority Doesn't Matter"

Each of these schools—arms control, hawkish, and academic—also differ on the impact and desirability of sharing dual-use nuclear technology for civilian applications. Obama administration officials insist that nuclear supplier states have an NPT obligation to transfer as much "peaceful" nuclear technology to nonweapons states as possible so long as it is for a declared civilian project that is internationally inspected. Failure to do so "without discrimination," in their eyes, risks unraveling the NPT.[22]

Most hawks, on the other hand, object to civilian nuclear cooperation with hostile states (e.g., Iran and North Korea) but otherwise support the global expansion of civilian nuclear power. They certainly are willing to share such technology with close friends even if such transfers might enhance existing or potential weapons options (e.g., India, South Korea, or Japan). As for the neorealists, some have faulted nuclear nonproliferation policies for unnecessarily inhibiting nuclear power's beneficial development domestically and overseas, but most have no set view.[23] Several have argued that letting nuclear weapons spread to selected countries or sharing "nuclear capabilities" with them might bolster U.S. security.[24]

---

*Political Science Quarterly* 94, no. 4, Winter 1979-80, pp. 617-633.

22. See note 5.

23. See e.g., Mueller, *Atomic Obsession*, pp. 138-141 and Steve Kidd, "Nuclear Proliferation Risk – Is It Vastly Overrated?" *Nuclear Engineering International*, July, 23 2010, available from *http://www.neimagazine.com/opinion/opinionnuclear-proliferation-risk-is-it-vastly-overrated/*.

24. See, e.g., Charles Kauthammer, "North Korea: Cold War Relic, Present Day Threat," *National Review Online*, January 5, 2017, available from *http://www.nationalreview.com/article/443592/north-korea-nuclear-program-threat-china-united-states*; Doug Bandow, "Letting South Korea Develop Nukes," *The Korea Times*, March 9, 2016, available from *http://www.koreatimes.co.kr/www/news/opinon/2016/03/197_199975.html*; Christine Leah, "Yes, Australia Still Needs Nukes: An Argument in Favor of Aussie Atom Bombs," *War is Boring*, January 2, 2016, available from *https://warisboring.com/yes-australia-still-needs-nukes-29f06bb7bbe#.10ue0wo84*; Harvey M. Sapolsky and Christine M. Leah,

For administration officials and arms control advocates, then, the superpowers must reduce their arsenals ("vertically") to encourage nonweapons states not to proliferate ("horizontally"). Failure at this risks instability or, worse, nuclear use. Hawkish critics, meanwhile, believe that reducing U.S. nuclear weapons capabilities is more likely to risk nuclear proliferation and war than otherwise would be the case if one augmented U.S. and allied strategic weapons capabilities or, at least, kept them from declining. Finally, academic skeptics deny that vertical reductions and horizontal nonproliferation are all that closely linked and suggest that more nuclear weapons in more hands may actually reduce the prospects

---

"Let Asia Go Nuclear," *The National Interest,* April 14, 2014, available from *http://nationalinterest.org/feature/let-asia-go-nuclear-10259*; Elbridge Colby, "Choose Geopolitics over Nonproliferation," *The National Interest,* February 28, 2014, available from *http://nationalinterest.org/commentary/choose-geopolitics-over-nonproliferation-9969*; Mark Helprin, "Why Israel Needs the Bomb," *Wall Street Journal,* October 18, 2010, available from *http://online.wsj.com/articles/SB1000142405274870367360457555002060636244;* John Mearsheimer, "Taiwan's Dire Straits," *The National Interest* no. 130, March/April 2014, pp. 29-39, available from *http://mearsheimer.uchicago.edu/pdfs/Taiwan's%20Dire%20Straits.pdf*; "The Case for a Ukrainian Nuclear Deterrent;" Rebecca Hersman, Clark A. Murdock, and Shanelle Van, *The Evolving U.S. Nuclear Narrative*, Washington DC: Center for Strategic and International Studies, November 1, 2016, available from *https://www.csis.org/analysis/evolving-us-nuclear-narrative-0*; and Clark Murdock and Thomas Karako, *Thinking about the Unthinkable in a Highly Proliferated World*, Washington DC: Center for Strategic and International Studies, July 2016, available from *https://www.csis.org/analysis/thinking-about-unthinkable-highly-proliferated-world*. It should be noted that these academic views have been reflected in the musings of both President Donald Trump during his 2016 campaign and British Foreign Minister Boris Johnson. See, "Transcript: Donald Trump Expounds on His Foreign Policy Views," *The New York Times*, March 26, 2016, available from *http://www.nytimes.com/2016/03/27/us/politics/donald-trump-transcript.html* and Boris Johnson, "Give Iran the bomb: it might make the regime more pliable," *The Telegraph*, October 12, 2006, available from *http://www.telegraph.co.uk/comment/personal-view/3633097/Give-Iran-the-bomb-it-might-make-the-regime-more-pliable.html*.

for war or, at the very least, that nuclear weapons and their proliferation are not all that significant (see Figure 1 on page 14 and 15).

# Figure 1.
# Nuclear Proliferation:  What We Think

| View | Selected Representatives | Favor Relying on Nuclear Weapons for Security |
|---|---|---|
| **Arms Control Perspective** | Most Western governments<br><br>International forums (e.g., IAEA, NPT Review Conference) | No |
| **Hawkish Supporters of Nuclear Weapons** | Nuclear weapons enthusiasts<br><br>Reagan-era Hawks (e.g., Donald Rumsfeld, Dick Cheney) | Yes |
| **Academic Skeptics/ Finite Deterrence Enthusiasts** | French Proponents of Force de Frappe & early backers of U.S. SLBM force (e.g., Pierre Gallois, Arleigh Burke)<br><br>Neorealists (e.g., Ken Waltz) | Yes |
| **Academic Skeptics/ Finite Deterrence Critics** | Post-neorealists (e.g., John Mueller) | No |

| Believe Nuclear Weapons Deter | Willing to Go to Zero | Support Sharing Civil Nuclear Energy | Support Sharing Nuclear Weapons-related Technology |
|---|---|---|---|
| Yes | Yes | Yes | No |
| Yes | No | Yes (for friends) No (for enemies) | Yes (to some friends) No (for enemies) |
| Yes | No | Unclear | Yes |
| No | Yes | Yes | No |

## *Reservations*

These three views on how nuclear weapons reductions and nonproliferation relate are clear, plausible, and popular. They dominate the current debate over nuclear weapons policies. There is only one problem: In practice, none of them make nearly as much sense as their supporters think.

One can see this most readily by examining how each school addresses the simplest and most popular of policy questions: Should one be for or against nuclear weapons? Add to this question (for the purposes of this inquiry) the matter of nuclear weapons proliferation, and the query admits to two simple answers—yes (in support of nuclear weapons and additional proliferation) or no against both.

Let's take the against-side first. Those opposed to nuclear weapons and their further proliferation—i.e., those who want to move toward zero nuclear weapons as soon as possible—go to great lengths to explain why a world without nuclear weapons is preferable to our current world. They emphasize Ronald Reagan's observation that a nuclear war can never be won and so should never be fought. They also detail how a world with zero nuclear weapons might work, and how one might prevent a relapse into a nuclear-armed world once nuclear weapons have been eliminated.[25]

Unfortunately, these same analysts are less articulate on how one might persuade existing nuclear weapons states to give up their weapons or how exactly one would get to zero.

---

25. See, e.g., George Perkovich and James M. Acton, *Abolishing Nuclear Weapons*, Adelphi Paper 396, London: International Institute for Strategic Studies, 2008; George P. Schultz, William J. Perry, Henry Kissinger, and Sam Nunn. "A World Free of Nuclear Weapons," *Wall Street Journal*, January 4, 2007, available from *http://online.wsj.com/article/SB116787515251566636.html*; and George P. Schultz, William J. Perry, Henry Kissinger, and Sam Nunn, "Toward a Nuclear-Free World," *Wall Street Journal*, January 15, 2008, available from *http://online.wsj.com/article/SB120036422673589947.html*.

So far, the United States and Russia have reduced their nuclear holdings from over 70,000 deployed nuclear weapons[26] to several thousand on each side.[27] This begs the question, though: How easy would it be to reduce further to a few hundred warheads if other states (e.g., China, Israel, France, the United Kingdom (UK), North Korea, Pakistan, or India) acquired or deployed as many or more? Would this not encourage increased military competitions, nuclear arms racing, miscalculation, and unnecessary, and potentially disastrous wars?

Securing clear answers to such questions, of course, is difficult. Nonetheless, analysts backing zero nuclear weapons offer a general picture of how things might work. According to their narrative, the more the U.S. government increases its support for nuclear weapons reductions and reduces its own arsenals with Russia, the more likely other nuclear-armed states (e.g., China, India, and Pakistan) would be to fall in line. To help promote this more restrained nuclear future, the United States and Russia, it is argued, should also abandon plans to deploy or defend their nuclear strategic forces in any effort to achieve military advantage over one another or other nations. Rather than aim their nuclear weapons against countless military targets, the superpowers should adopt finite nuclear deterrence strategies that would hold each other's population and industrial centers at risk. Defending these cities and military assets should also be eschewed in order to assure mutual vulnerability.

---

26. See Natural Resources Defense Council, "Table of Global Nuclear Weapons Stockpiles, 1945-2002," available from *http://www.nrdc.org/nuclear/nudb/datab19.asp*, last updated November 25, 2002 and Robert S. Norris and Hans M. Kristensen, "Global Nuclear Weapons Inventories, 1945-2013," *Bulletin of the Atomic Scientists* 69, no. 5, September/October 2013, pp. 75-81, available from *http://bos.sagepub.com/content/69/5/75.full*.

27. See U.S. Department of State, "New START Treaty Aggregate Numbers of Strategic Offensive Arms," Fact Sheet, April 1, 2016, available from *https://web.archive.org/web/20170108180000/https://www.state.gov/t/avc/rls/2016/255377.htm*.

This would reduce the need for ever larger, more accurate, quick-alert nuclear arsenals and make deep cuts in existing nuclear stockpiles more feasible. With increased nuclear restraint by the major nuclear states, states lacking nuclear weapons would become more willing to eschew nuclear weapons and support nuclear nonproliferation.[28]

This is the upbeat narrative. The downbeat narrative has us clinging to our bombs. The more we maintain our nuclear stockpiles, we are warned, the more it will undermine our claims that we want to rely less on nuclear arms to assure our security. This, in turn, risks encouraging other states to acquire nuclear weapons (i.e., promoting more North Koreas, Irans, and Pakistans), which will only strain existing security relations and tempt America's friends and allies (e.g., South Korea, Japan, Saudi Arabia, Turkey, etc.) to acquire nuclear weapons options of their own.

Those backing nuclear reductions also offer historical analysis to challenge the presumed security utility of nuclear weapons. Nuclear arms, they note, have failed to deter important conventional wars (e.g., the Korean or Vietnam wars or the Egyptian strike against

---

28. See e.g., Gareth Evans and Yoriko Kawaguchi, *Eliminating Nuclear Threats: A Practical Agenda for Global Policymakers,* Canberra: International Commission on Nuclear Non-proliferation and Disarmament, 2009, available from *http://icnnd.org/Reference/reports/ent/downloads.html*; Bruce Blair, et al., "Smaller and Safer," *Foreign Affairs* 89, no. 5, September-October 2010, available from *http://www.foreignaffairs.com/articles/66540/bruce-blair-victor-esin-matthew-mckinzie-valery-yarynich-and-pav/smaller-and-safer*; Gen. (Ret.) James Cartwright, et. al., *Global Zero U.S. Nuclear Policy Commission Report: Modernizing U.S. Nuclear Strategy, Force Structure and Posture,* Global Zero, May 2012, available from *http://www.globalzero.org/files/gz_us_nuclear_policy_commission_report.pdf*; and Deep Cuts Commission, *Preparing for Deep Cuts: Options for Enhancing Euro-Atlantic and International Security,* First Report of the Deep Cuts Commission, Hamburg: Institute for Peace Research and Security Policy at the University of Hamburg, April 2014, available from *http://www.cissm.umd.edu/publications/preparing-deep-cuts-options-enhancing-euro-atlantic-and-international-security-0*.

Israel in '73) or terrorist attacks (e.g., 9/11 and the Pakistani-backed terrorist strikes against targets in India and Afghanistan).

Attempts to acquire nuclear weapons, as well as mere possession, also have prompted military strikes (e.g., Iran, Israel, and the United States against Iraq's nuclear reactor at Osirak in 1980, 1981, 1991, and 2002; Iraq against Iran's reactor at Bushehr in repeated attacks from 1984-1988; Iraq's failed Scud missile strike against Israel's reactor at Dimona in 1991; and Israel's strike against Syria's reactor in 2007). In addition, attacks were seriously considered against new nuclear states (e.g., the United States against the Soviet Union in 1949 and the Soviet Union against China in 1969).[29] Bottom line: The possession and spread of nuclear weapons generally undermines security. What, then, are nuclear weapons good for? Only the peculiar task of deterring other states from using their nuclear weapons.

This last reflection, of course, is intended to further demonstrate how little value nuclear weapons add and why their early elimination is desired. This conclusion, though, is triple-edged. Certainly, if nuclear weapons truly are not all that militarily valuable, what is the urgency to eliminate them? Some states held on to their horse cavalries after the First World War and their battleships long after the Second World War, but that hardly encouraged their rivals to acquire them, and by mid-century these military instruments hardly posed a strategic threat to anyone.

On the other hand, if nuclear weapons can effectively deter other nuclear-armed states, wouldn't that make their acquisition by non-

---

29. See Matthew Fuhrmann, "Preventive War and the Spread of Nuclear Programs," in *Moving Beyond Pretense: Nuclear Power and Nonproliferation*, ed. Henry Sokolski, Carlisle, PA: Strategic Studies Institute, 2014, pp. 91-115, available from *http://www.npolicy.org/books/Moving_Beyond_Pretense/Ch4_Fuhrmann.pdf*.

weapons states all but irresistible?  The refrain of many security analysts after the first Gulf War against Iraq was that the United States would never have tried to remove Saddam Hussein if he actually had the bomb.  In what way were they wrong?

Finally, is it reasonable to think that no one will ever use their nuclear weapons first?  Don't states that believe in nuclear deterrence presume that if they lacked a survivable nuclear deterrent, their nuclear adversaries might strike their or their allies' vulnerable forces in an attempt to gain some clear advantage?  If so, wouldn't they constantly (and naturally) be worried that their or their allies' nuclear retaliatory capabilities might be knocked out or be seriously degraded in a first strike by their opponents?  Wouldn't failing to attend to these matters and merely making bluffs to retaliate against a few targets of dubious military value (e.g., large population centers versus strategic weapons bases) risk making a hash of the whole notion of deterrence?[30]

If you allowed, as one should, that the answers to these questions are, at least, unclear, you would expect lengthy, heated debate about what the answers might be.  What's telling, however, is how little debate there is.  Instead, if these issues are raised at all, the subject of conversation invariably is shifted to a much less contentious set of concerns: The horrors of nuclear theft, nuclear accidents, unauthorized use, sabotage, and terrorism.  Focusing on these issues quickly brings one to the desired conclusion (again) that the immediate reduction of nuclear weapons would immediately make for a much safer world.[31]  In the interim, we need to do all we can to increase

---

30. On these points see Michael Quinlin, "Easements and Escape Routes," *Thinking About Nuclear Weapons,* Oxford: Oxford University Press, 2009, pp. 99-111.

31. See, e.g., James E. Doyle, "Why Eliminate Nuclear Weapons?" *Survival* 55, no. 1, February-March 2013, pp. 7-34, available from *http://www.iiss.org/en/ publications/survival/sections/2013-94b0/survival--global-politics-and-strategy-*

security over existing nuclear weapons assets and reduce the readiness and numbers of deployed nuclear forces to head off these possible threats.

Most of these nuclear security concerns are necessarily speculative. Neither accidental nor unauthorized nuclear use has yet occurred. Yet, there *is* plenty of near history (close calls of Russian, South African, French, Chinese, and American nuclear launches, tests, and thefts, Broken Arrow incidents, provocative nuclear tests, "lost" warheads, and nuclear weapons-usable materials gone unaccounted for).[32] As for preventing acts of nuclear terrorism, though, such efforts are entirely anticipatory: Specific, validated intelligence regarding acts of nuclear terrorism has, so far, gone wanting.[33]

---

*february-march-2013-3db7/55-1-02-doyle-a88b.* Mr. Doyle challenges the security utility of nuclear deterrence and argues that accidental use, nuclear terrorism, and the probability of deterrence failure--recommend the elimination of nuclear weapons.

32. See Henry D. Sokolski and Bruno Tertrais, eds., *Nuclear Weapons Security Crises: What Does History Teach?* Carlisle, PA: Strategic Studies Institute, 2013; Ed Pilkington, "US nearly detonated atomic bomb over North Carolina – secret document," *Guardian* (Manchester), September 20, 2013, available from *http://www.theguardian.com/world/2013/sep/20/usaf-atomic-bomb-north-carolina-1961*; Michael Winter, "Report: Nuke that fell on N.C. in 1961 almost exploded," *USA Today*, September 20, 2013, available from *http://www.usatoday.com/story/news/nation/2013/09/20/north-carolina-atomic-bomb/2845381/*; "Lost nuclear weapons are an unreported problem," *NJ Today.net*, February 24, 2016, available from *http://njtoday.net/2016/02/24/lost-nuclear-weapons-are-an-unreported-problem/*; and Peter Burt, *Playing With Fire: Nuclear Weapons Incidents and Accidents in the United Kingdom*, Reading, UK: Nuclear Information Service, February 2017, available from *http://nuclearinfo.org/article/nis-reports/playing-fire-nuclear-weapons-incidents-and-accidents-united-kingdom*. For much more comprehensive analyses see Eric Schlosser, *Command and Control: Nuclear Weapons, the Damascus Accident and the Illusion of Safety,* New York: Penguin Press, 2013 and Scott D. Sagan, *The Limits of Safety: Organizations, Accidents, and Nuclear Weapons,* Princeton, NJ: Princeton University Press, 1993.

33. At least this was so up through 2010 when The Commission on the Prevention

Despite this (or, perhaps, because of it), addressing these threats has become a public policy cause célèbre. Today, nuclear terrorism is viewed by both Republican and Democratic officials as the "most immediate and extreme" threat facing America and the world.[34] Bil-

---

of WMD Proliferation and Terrorism, which I served on as a member, concluded its work. The commission originally set out to demonstrate that nuclear terrorism was the most pressing threat to the U.S. After seeking and failing to find any validated, specific intelligence on any known nuclear terrorist threats, however, the commission shifted its focus to bioterrorism, which included the celebrated anthrax letter attacks of September 18, 2001. As for the possible hand off of nuclear arms to terrorists, even those most eager to focus U.S. efforts against nuclear terrorism downplay this threat. See, e.g., Travis Sharp and Erica Poff, "Understanding and Preventing Nuclear Terrorism," *The Center for Arms Control and Non-proliferation*, December 3, 2008, available from *research.policyarchive. org/11818.pdf* and Keir A. Lieber and Daryl Press, "Why States Won't Give Nuclear Weapons to Terrorists," *International Security* 38, no. 1, Summer 2013, pp. 80-104, available from *http://belfercenter.ksg.harvard.edu/files/IS3801_pp080-104. pdf*. Much more plausible is the risk that governments might lose control of their nuclear weapons assets to illegitimate factions operating within their government, or that civilian or military nuclear facilities might be sabotaged particularly in unstable regions of the Middle and Far East. The first, though, is not a terrorist problem per se and the second does not threaten nuclear use. On these risks, see Edwin Lyman, "Nuclear Plant Protection and the Homeland Security Mandate," paper prepared for Institute of Nuclear Materials Management 44th Annual Meeting, Phoenix, AZ, July 13-17, 2003, available from *http://nuclear-power-security.blogspot.com/2007/03/nuclear-plant-protection-and-homeland_02.html*; Bruno Tertrais, "The Unexpected Risk: The Impact of Political Crises on the Security and Control of Nuclear Weapons," in *Nuclear Weapons Security Crises*, pp. 3-22, available from *http://npolicy.org/books/Security_Crises/Ch1_Tertrais. pdf*; and Alissa J. Rubin and Milan Schreuer, "Belgium Fears Nuclear Plants Are Vulnerable," *The New York Times*, March 25, 2016, available from *http://www.nytimes.com/2016/03/26/world/europe/belgium-fears-nuclear-plants-are-vulnerable.html*.

34. See "Remarks by President Barack Obama," Hradcany Square, Prague, Czech Republic, April 5, 2009. President George W. Bush said that nuclear weapons falling "in the hands of a terrorist enemy" is the single most serious threat the security of the United States. In "The First Bush-Kerry Presidential Debate," The Commission on Presidential Debates, September 30, 2004, transcript available from *http://www.debates.org/index.php?page=september-30-2004-debate-transcript*. Senator John Kerry, Democratic Presidential Nominee in 2004,

lions of dollars are appropriated annually on questionable nuclear weapons detection and forensics efforts and nuclear security and cooperative threat reduction programs.[35] Meanwhile, broad intelligence sweeps, including of domestic phone and internet communications, have been justified, in no small part, to prevent possible terrorist use of weapons of mass destruction.[36]

---

remarked in a campaign speech that "the possibility of al Qaeda or other terrorists getting their hands on a nuclear weapon" was the "greatest threat we face today" See "New Strategies to Meet New Threats," Remarks of John Kerry, June 1, 2004, in Gerhard Peters and John T. Woolley, eds., *The American Presidency Project,* available from *http://www.presidency.ucsb.edu/ws/?pid=29697.* Also see Graham Allison, "Nuclear Terrorism Poses the Gravest Threat Today," *Wall Street Journal,* July 14, 2003, available from *http://online.wsj.com/news/articles/SB105813273777796800.* For a contrarian view, see Leonard Weiss, "On Fear and Nuclear Terrorism," *Bulletin of the Atomic Scientists* 71, no. 2, March 2015, pp. 75-87; Brian Jenkins, *Will Terrorists Go Nuclear?* New York: Prometheus Books, 2008; and Brian Jenkins, "Nuclear Terrorism, the Last 40 Years: What Has and Has Not Happened," in Henry Sokolski, ed., *The Nuclear Terrorism Threat: How Real Is It?* Arlington, VA: The Nonproliferation Policy Education Center, 2016, available from *http://npolicy.org/article_file/1602_Jenkins.pdf.*

35. See, e.g., Gina Page, "U.S. Borders Flunk Smuggling Test," *CBS News,* March 27, 2006, available from *http://www.cbsnews.com/news/us-borders-flunk-smuggling-test/*; Richard Weitz, "Nuclear Forensics: False Hopes and Practical Realities," *Political Science Quarterly* 126, no. 1, Spring 2011, pp. 53-75; U.S. Government Accountability Office, *Nuclear Detection: Domestic Nuclear Detection Office Should Improve Planning to Better Address Gaps and Vulnerabilities,* GAO-09-257, Washington, DC: GPO, March 2, 2009, available from *http://www.gao.gov/products/GAO-09-257*; *Combating Nuclear Smuggling: Lessons Learned from Cancelled Radiation Portal Monitor Program Could Help Future Acquisitions,* GAO-13-256, Washington, DC: GPO, May 2013, available from *http://www.gao.gov/products/gao-13-256*; and Anthony Kimery, "Risks Posed By Foreign Ports Shipping Cargo to U.S. Not Adequately Assessed, GAO, Authorities Say," *Homeland Security Today,* September 30, 2013, available from *http://www.hstoday.us/index.php?id=483&cHash=081010&tx_ttnews%5Btt_news%5D=32913.*

36. See Eric Lichtblau, "In Secret, Court Vastly Broadens Powers of NSA," *The New York Times,* July 6, 2013, available from *http://www.nytimes.com/2013/07/07/us/in-secret-court-vastly-broadens-powers-of-nsa.html?pagewanted=all&_r=0* and Ken Dilanian, "Intelligence Leakers Post 'Critical Threat' to U.S.,

Far less controversial are the international nuclear security summits President Obama launched in 2009. The fourth, held in Washington D.C. in 2016, allowed scores of nations, including those acquiring or deploying nuclear weapons, to extol the virtues of keeping their nuclear weapons-related assets safe against seizure, sabotage, and illicit use. Details about how they might accomplish this, however, were kept, as with previous summits, to a minimum, lest hostile states learn what might be needed to attack or seize these holdings.

Although this set of nuclear security worries has been spotlighted to maximize alarm, many who voice them are nonetheless convinced that further progress on nuclear arms control, which would eliminate most of these problems, is all but inevitable. They celebrate the New START (Strategic Arms Reduction Treaty) agreement and are enthusiastic about reaching further unilateral and negotiated cuts as well as ratification of the Comprehensive Nuclear-Test-Ban Treaty (CTBT).[37] They also remain steadfast in their belief that negotiated settlements can roll back Iran's and North Korea's "aberrant" nucle-

---

Say Spy Chiefs," *Los Angeles Times*, January 29, 2014, available from *http://articles.latimes.com/2014/jan/29/world/la-fg-wn-us-intelligence-snowden-leakers-threat-20140129*. See also the reaction to the recommendations within a recent Defense Science Board Task Force Report in U.S. Department of Defense, Defense Science Board, *Assessment of Nuclear Monitoring and Verification Technologies,* Washington, DC: Office of the Under Secretary of Defense for Acquisition, Technology and Logistics, January 2014, available from *http://www.acq.osd.mil/dsb/reports/NuclearMonitoringAndVerificationTechnologies.pdf* and Siobhan Gorman, "Panel Calls for More Spy Capability: NSA Cited as Model in Monitoring Nuclear Threats," *Wall Street Journal*, January 21, 2014, available from *http://www.wsj.com/news/articles/SB10001424052702304027204579335120352342540*.

37. See, e.g., R. Jeffrey Smith, "Obama Administration Embraces Major New Nuclear Weapons Cut*,"* *Center for Public Integrity*, February 8, 2013, available from *http://www.publicintegrity.org/2013/02/08/12156/obama-administration-embraces-major-new-nuclear-weapons-cut* and Daryl G. Kimball, "Obama's Second Chance," *Arms Control Today* 43, no. 1, January-February 2013, available from *https://www.armscontrol.org/act/2013_01-02/Focus*.

ar misbehavior. Yet, little is said about other nuclear or near-nuclear weapons states. Instead, there is self-congratulation that President John F. Kennedy's earlier warnings that there might be 20 or more nuclear weapons states by 1970[38] proved to be unfounded and insistence that pushing more arms control is our best hope to eliminate the remaining nuclear threat.

What else must be pursued besides more START negotiations and nuclear security summits? Three things, all of which President Obama announced in his 2009 Prague speech: Bring the CTBT and Fissile Material Cut-off Treaty (FMCT) into force and share "peaceful" civilian nuclear technology under appropriate international safeguards. This roughly tracks the now popular "three-pillar" view of the NPT—that to get nonweapons states not to acquire nuclear weapons, the weapons states must reduce their nuclear arms and offer more "peaceful" nuclear energy transfers.

Putting aside the improbability of the U.S. Senate or Moscow backing the ratification of more significant arms control agreements any time soon, accomplishing this agenda is practically impossible without the unlikely support of states such as Iran, North Korea, Pakistan, India, Israel, and Egypt. More important, some of the objections to these agreements are not merely political, but substantive.[39]

---

38. John F. Kennedy, "Speech at State Department Auditorium," Speech, Washington D.C., March 21, 1963, available from *https://www.jfklibrary.org/Research/Research-Aids/Ready-Reference/Press-Conferences/News-Conference-52.aspx*.

39. Several arms control critics have noted that nuclear testing may not be necessary for initial weapons acquisition and that what constitutes a test may be in disagreement among those that have signed the CTBT. See Jonathan Medalia, "Comprehensive Nuclear-test-ban Treaty: Issues and Arguments," CRS Report for Congress, RL 34494, Washington, DC: Congressional Research Service, March 12, 2008, pp. 20-22, available from *http://www.fas.org/sgp/crs/nuke/RL34394.pdf*; U.S. Congressional Commission on the Strategic Posture of the United States, *America's Strategic Posture,* Washington, DC: United States

As for sharing "peaceful" nuclear technology and disarming to secure continued nonproliferation, it is difficult to see how such an approach can prevent future Indias, Irans, Syrias, or North Koreas. Even if one ignores how little of the NPT's diplomatic history actually supports today's legalistic enthusiasm for the "three-pillar" view,[40] promoting this bargain is, at best, problematic.

---

Institute of Peace Press, 2009, p. 83, available from *http://www.usip.org/sites/default/files/America's_Strategic_Posture_Auth_Ed.pdf*; Keith B. Payne and R. James Woolsey, "Reconsidering the Comprehensive Test Ban Treaty," *National Review Online*, September 8, 2011, available from *http://www.nationalreview.com/article/276530/reconsidering-comprehensive-test-ban-treaty-r-james-woolsey-keith-b-payne*; and Kathleen Bailey, et al., *The Comprehensive Test Ban Treaty: An Assessment of the Benefits, Costs, and Risks*, Fairfax, VA: National Institute Press, 2010, available from *http://www.nipp.org/wp-content/uploads/2014/12/CTBT-3.11.11-electronic-version.pdf*. Several of these critics also note that the current versions of the FMCT do not address civilian production that could be easily diverted to make bombs nor does it address past fissile production. See, e.g., Christopher A. Ford, "Five Plus Three: How to Have a Meaningful and Helpful Fissile Material Cutoff Treaty," *Arms Control Today* 39, no. 2, March 29, 2009, available from *http://legacy.armscontrol.org/act/2009_03/Ford* and Idem., "The United States and the Fissile Material Cutoff Treaty," Paper presented to the "Preparing for 2010: Getting the Process Right" conference, Annecy, France, March 17, 2007, available from *http://2001-2009.state.gov/t/isn/rls/other/81950.htm*.

40. See Albert Wohlstetter, "Spreading the Bomb without Quite Breaking the Rules," *Foreign Policy*, no. 25, Winter 1976-77, pp. 88-94, 145-179, available from *http://www.npolicy.org/userfiles/file/Nuclear%20Heuristics-Spreading%20the%20Bomb%20without%20Quite%20Breaking%20the%20Rules.pdf*; Arthur Steiner, "Article IV and the 'Straightforward Bargain,'" PAN Heuristics Paper 78-832-08, in Albert Wohlstetter, et al., *Towards a New Consensus on Nuclear Technology*, Vol. II, Supporting Papers, ACDA Report No. PH-78-04-832-33, Marina del Rey, CA: PAN Heuristics, 1978, pp. 1-8; Eldon V.C. Greenberg, *The NPT and Plutonium: Application of NPT Prohibitions to "Civilian" Nuclear Equipment, Technology and Materials Associated with Reprocessing and Plutonium Use*, Washington, DC: The Nuclear Control Institute, 1993, available from *http://npolicy.org/books/Reviewing_NPT/Ch6_Greenberg.pdf*; Henry Sokolski, "The Nuclear Nonproliferation Treaty and Peaceful Nuclear Energy," Testimony before "Assessing 'Rights' under the Nuclear Nonproliferation Treaty," a hearing of the U.S. House of Representatives, Committee on International

First, although encouraging nuclear weapons restraint can indirectly support nonproliferation, it is unclear how insisting on making nuclear disarmament a legally binding quid pro quo for adopting sound nonproliferation measures would work. In practice, nonweapons states have held their adoption of nonproliferation measures hostage to the superpowers doing more to disarm while their claim of insufficient progress on this front gives them a diplomatic pretext to threaten to acquire nuclear weapons themselves. From a nuclear control perspective, none of this is helpful. Backing off necessary nonproliferation controls only increases the prospects for more nuclear weapons proliferation. This, in turn, is only likely to increase demand for more nuclear armament.

Second, it is unclear how supplying nonweapons states with the benefits of truly "peaceful" nuclear technology could assist in promoting more or tighter nonproliferation controls. If the technology in question is genuinely benign, by definition, it ought to be easy to safeguard effectively against military diversions and so be safe to share free of any apprehensions it might be diverted to make bombs. If, furthermore, the nuclear item in question is profitable to sell, it is difficult to understand why nuclear supplier states would need additional incentives, much less nonproliferation ones, to share it.

---

Relations, Subcommittee on International Terrorism and Nonproliferation, March 2, 2006, available from *http://www.npolicy.org/article.php?aid=392&rtid=8*; Robert Zarate, "The Three Qualifications of Article IV's 'Inalienable Right'" and Christopher Ford, "Nuclear Technology Rights and Wrongs: The NPT, Article IV, and Nonproliferation," in Henry Sokolski, ed., *Reviewing the NPT,* Carlisle, PA: Strategic Studies Institute, 2010, pp. 219-384, available from *http://npolicy.org/books/Reviewing_NPT/Ch11_Ford.pdf*; and Dean Rust, "How We've Come to View the NPT: Three Pillars," in Henry Sokolski, ed., *Nuclear Rules, Not Just Rights: The NPT Reexamined*, Arlington, VA: The Nonproliferation Policy Education Center, 2017, available from *http://npolicy.org/books/Nuclear_Rules_Not_Just_Rights/Ch2_Rust.pdf*.

On the other hand, if what was being sold is proliferation-prone (i.e., close and essential to bomb-making) and, therefore, dangerous to share, it is unclear why any state eager to promote nuclear nonproliferation would think it had an NPT obligation to transfer it. Again, effective nuclear nonproliferation presumes the sharing of only truly "peaceful" nuclear goods and technologies—i.e., of nuclear items and know-how that are so far from making bombs that attempts to divert them for this purpose could be detected early and reliably enough to intervene effectively to prevent any weapons from ever being built. The alternative would be that there is an NPT obligation to share dangerous nuclear technologies and goods that can bring a nonweapons state to the very brink of acquiring bombs. But how much nonproliferation sense would that make? The answer is all too clear.

This, then, brings us to hawks who object to such wishful thinking—those who are "for" nuclear weapons. Their brief essentially is that nuclear weapons have kept the peace. If you push for deeper nuclear reductions, they argue, it will do nothing to slow determined proliferators from acquiring nuclear weapons.[41] More important, it could undermine our security alliance system, which, in turn, would increase the risks that our friends and allies might go nuclear.[42] All of this, in turn, would only increase the prospects for war and the possible use of nuclear weapons.

---

41. See, c.f., Stuart Colin, "A Nuclear Earthquake: The Case Against Unilateral Disarmament," *Foreign Affairs Review*, October 25, 2016, available from *http://foreignaffairsreview.co.uk/2016/10/a-nuclear-earthquake-the-case-against-unilateral-disarmament/*; Stephen Rademaker, "Blame America First," *Wall Street Journal*, May 7, 2007, available from *http://online.wsj.com/news/articles/SB117849961888494020/*; and Kyle Mizokami, "Obama Administration Cuts Back Size of Nuclear Arsenal," *Popular Mechanics*, January 12, 2017, available from *http://www.popularmechanics.com/military/weapons/a24739/obama-administration-unilateral-nuclear-arms-cuts/*.

42. See e.g., Josh Rogin, "Exclusive: House Republicans Ding Obama on Nuke Treaty in Previously Unreported Letter," *Foreign Policy, The Cable*, September

This line of argument, like that of the zero nuclear weapons crowd, makes a number of sensible points. Yet, it too is imperfect. First, as has already been noted, we know that nuclear weapons have not deterred all wars. Both North Korea and North Vietnam took the United States on in long-fought wars. Nor did U.S. nuclear weapons deter China and Russia from lending Hanoi and Pyongyang substantial military support.[43] Then there's the Israeli war of 1973. Israeli possession of nuclear arms may have changed the way the war was fought (the United States finally came to Israel's aid at the last moment for fear that the war might go nuclear). But Israeli nuclear weapons did not prevent the war.[44] Finally, it is unclear how, if at all, nuclear weapons might deter nonstate actors from engaging in terrorism—nuclear or nonnuclear.[45]

---

16, 2009, available from *http://thecable.foreignpolicy.com/posts/2009/09/16/exclusive_house_republicans_ding_obama_on_nuke_treaty_in_previously_unreported_lett*.

43. See, e.g., Carl A. Posey, "How the Korean War Almost Went Nuclear," *Air and Space Smithsonian*, July 2015, available from *http://www.airspacemag.com/military-aviation/how-korean-war-almost-went-nuclear-180955324/*; Bernard Gwertzman, *The New York Times*, "US Papers Tell of '53 Policy to Use A-Bomb in Korea," June 8, 1984, available from *http://www.nytimes.com/1984/06/08/world/us-papers-tell-of-53-policy-to-use-a-bomb-in-korea.html*; William Burr and Jeffrey Kimball, "Nixon White House Considered Nuclear Options Against North Vietnam, Declassified Documents Reveal," *National Security Archive Electronic Briefing Book No. 195*, posted July 31, 2006, available from *http://nsarchive.gwu.edu/NSAEBB/NSAEBB195/*; and Fredrick Logevall, "We Might Give Them a Few," Did the US Offer to Drop Atom Bombs at Dien Bien Phu?" *The Bulletin of Atomic Scientists*, February 21, 2016, available from *http://thebulletin.org/we-might-give-them-few-did-us-offer-drop-atom-bombs-dien-bien-phu9175*.

44. See Shlomo Brom, "Utility of Nuclear Deterrence in the Middle East," and Karim Haggag, "Proliferation and Deterrence beyond the Nuclear Tipping Point in the Middle East" in George P. Shultz and James E. Goodby, eds., *The War that Must Never Be Fought: Dilemmas of Nuclear Deterrence*, Stanford, CA: Hoover Institution Press, 2015, pp. 221-223 and 235-243.

45. In the case of nonnuclear terrorism, Pakistani-backed terror strikes against

Perhaps the point is nuclear weapons have prevented some "major" (nuclear) wars or "major" defeats rather than all forms of military aggression. This seems plausible. Certainly, the number of war casualties as a percentage of the world's population has declined significantly since Hiroshima and Nagasaki.[46] Yet, any "proof" of why something didn't happen can never be known with scientific certainty. As we have discussed, a good number of security experts question if nuclear deterrence ever really "worked" during the Cold War.[47] Nor is the threat of nuclear escalation the only possible expla-

---

India suggest nuclear deterrence against such threats is hardly effective. Hawkish defenders of nuclear deterrence insist that given the heavy state sponsorship of nonstate actors, though, nuclear threats properly focused could, in some cases, help deter WMD terrorism. See, e.g., Brad Roberts, "Deterrence and WMD Terrorism: Calibrating Its Potential Contributions to Risk Reduction," IDA Paper P-4231, Institute for Defense Analyses, Alexandria, VA, June 2007. That said, no act of terrorism involving the detonation of a nuclear weapon has yet been seriously attempted.

46. For a graphic analysis of this last point, see Admiral Richard Mies, USN (ret.), "Strategic Deterrence in the 21st Century," *Undersea Warfare*, no. 48, Spring 2012, pp. 12-19, available from *http://www.public.navy.mil/subfor/ underseawarfaremagazine/Issues/PDF/USW_Spring_2012.pdf* and Adam Lowther, "The Nation's Ultimate Insurance Policy: Nuclear Weapons," *Real Clear Defense,* May 16, 2016, available from *http://www.realcleardefense. com/articles/2016/05/16/the_nations_ultimate_insurance_policy_nuclear_ weapons_109364.html.*

47. See e.g., Steven P. Lee, *Morality, Prudence, and Nuclear Weapons,* Cambridge Studies in Philosophy and Public Policy, Cambridge: Cambridge University Press, 1993. It's well to keep in mind that a nuclear deterrence effort might fail to prevent a particular act of aggression or some other undesirable event because of some deficiency in the nuclear deterrent force or the manner in which the nuclear threat itself was made. The challenge nuclear deterrence presents for security analysts, then, is determining what, if any, impact it has had in the past and is likely to have in the future. Unfortunately, posing this question is all too similar to the illicit mathematical operation of dividing an integer by zero: It immediately produces an infinite number of possible answers. This suggests two possibilities. The first is that nuclear deterrence is a myth that should be disregarded. The second is that whatever people think the specific impact of nuclear deterrence is, is itself a political military reality that must be dealt with—whether the view held

nation for why post-WWII war casualties declined so much (smaller wars usually follow large ones; post-war alliances were created and kept strong; military science improved; with lower aiming inaccuracies, indiscriminate damage in war declined, etc.) These other explanations certainly cannot be entirely discounted.

This, then, brings us to the second problem—this argument's lack of qualification. If one allows that nuclear weapons have deterred major wars, what is one to make of the observation? If some nuclear weapons have deterred some wars, wouldn't more deter more and wouldn't more advanced (or, at least, an ability to produce them quickly) deter even more?[48] Wouldn't this recommend increasing nuclear production capacities and resuming nuclear testing?[49] Also, what of other states that lack such arms? Wouldn't

---

is itself sound or not. In either case, the general concept of nuclear deterrence (as distinct from the key technical requirements for effective, affordable, and survivable nuclear forces) is something that is less than a science.

48. On the desirability of being able to "adapt" the size and character of one's nuclear weapons force quickly and of redeploying U.S. tactical nuclear weapons overseas, see Keith B. Payne, et al., *Nuclear Force Adaptability for Deterrence and Assurance: A Prudent Alternative to Minimum Deterrence,* Fairfax, VA: National Institute Press, 2014, available from *http://www.nipp.org/wp-content/uploads/2014/12/MD-II-for-web.pdf* and Clark Murdoch et al., *Project Atom: A Competitive Strategies Approach to Defining U.S. Nuclear Strategy and Posture for 2025-2050*, CSIS Reports, Center for Strategic & International Studies, May 2015, available from *http://csis.org/files/publication/150601_Murdock_ProjectAtom_Web.pdf.*

49. See, e.g., Matthew Kroenig, "Trump Said the U.S. Should Expand Nuclear Weapons. He's Right.," *Politico,* December 23, 2016, available from *http://www.politico.com/magazine/story/2016/12/trump-said-the-us-should-expand-nuclear-weapons-hes-right-214546*; Robert R. Monroe, "Trump Should Change U.S. Policy On Nuclear Weapons," *Investors Business Daily,* December 16, 2016, available from *http://www.investors.com/politics/commentary/trump-should-change-u-s-policy-on-nuclear-weapons/*; Michaela Dodge and Brett Schaefer, "Rejection of UN Nuke Ban Not Enough, Administration Must Do More to Maintain Arsenal," *The Daily Signal,* October 31, 2016, available from *http://dailysignal.com/2016/10/31/rejection-of-un-nuke-ban-not-enough-*

their acquisition of nuclear forces help deter wars as well? Might the further proliferation of weapons, at least to our friends, then, be a good thing? Vice President Richard "Dick" Cheney argued that if China failed to get North Korea to eliminate its nuclear weapons capabilities, it might well prompt Japan to acquire nuclear weapons of its own. Donald Trump has argued that Japan and South Korea will eventually go nuclear and this may be good; Boris Johnson that helping Iran get the bomb might bolster peace. One also hears hawkish American support for Israel maintaining its nuclear forces until there is peace in the Middle East and for India to build its nuclear capabilities up to counter China's nuclear forces.[50]

As logically consistent as these arguments may be, they ought to cause unease. An unspoken assumption is that nuclear deterrence will work perfectly (as it supposedly did with Russia during the Cold War) and that it can be counted upon to work perfectly forever into the future. This is presumed no matter how many nuclear-armed states there might be, how rash or reckless these countries' leaders are, or how vulnerable their forces might be to a first strike. It also presumes, *sub silentio*, that the lack of truly disastrous nuclear weapons accidents, unauthorized firings, acts of nuclear terrorism, and thefts that we have experienced so far is a permanent feature.[51] All of this might well be correct in the near

---

*administration-must-do-more-to-maintain-arsenal/*; Frank Gaffney, "Fight Nuclear Provocation with Nuclear Provocation," transcript, Secure Freedom Minute, April 24, 2014, available from *http://www.breitbart.com/Breitbart-TV/2014/04/24/Gaffney-Fight-Nuclear-Provocation-With-Nuclear-Provocation*; and Jon Kyl, "Why We Need to Test Nuclear Weapons," *The Wall Street Journal*, October 20, 2009, available from *http://www.wsj.com/articles/SB10001424052748704500604574483224117732120*.

50. See note 24.

51. Recent analysis of past U.S. and Soviet nuclear accidents suggests the size of these two states' arsenals hardly correlated to the number of nuclear accidents. In fact, historically the correlation has been negative. What is unknown, however, is how well other countries have secured their arsenals against theft and accidents,

and mid-term. But barring the adoption of new, more effective nuclear restraints and security controls that apply not just to the United States, but to other nations, it is difficult to believe such optimism is much more than a bet against the house.

Yet another unspoken premise at play is that smaller nuclear weapons states and states eager to develop a nuclear weapons option are merely "lesser included threats." The notion here is that if the United States can deter or constrain Russia, the largest nuclear weapons state, the United States and its allies are safe (or much safer) against any other lesser nuclear-armed state. This roughly was the message in the 2012 presidential election campaign when candidate Mitt Romney described Russia as America's number one geopolitical foe and the Obama administration defended the primacy of working with Russia (versus China or other smaller nuclear states) to limit America's nuclear arsenal. Russia is our most important strategic competitor.[52] Deal with it and you can deal with

---

what their history has been and what it and the history of U.S. nuclear weapons accidents will be. In this regard, only one large accident is needed to change history forever. Thus, our experience so far is not necessarily dispositive. Compare note 32 with Keith Payne, et al., *Minimum Deterrence: Examining the Evidence,* Fairfax, VA: National Institute Press, 2013, pp. 52-54, available from *http://www.nipp.org/wp-content/uploads/2014/12/Final-Distro.pdf.* Also consider "Lost nuclear weapons are an unreported problem," *NJ Today,* February 24, 2016, available from *http://njtoday.net/2016/02/24/lost-nuclear-weapons-are-an-unreported-problem/.*

52. For a fulsome discussion of campaign comments made by Romney and Obama on these issues, see Molly Moorhead, "Obama: Romney Called Russia Our Top Geopolitical Threat," October 22, 2012, available from *http://www.politifact.com/truth-o-meter/statements/2012/oct/22/barack-obama/obama-romney-called-russia-our-top-geopolitical-fo/* and Matt Spetalnick and Jeremy Laurence, "Obama Vows to Pursue Further Nuclear Cuts with Russia," *Reuters,* March 26, 2012, available from *http://www.reuters.com/article/2012/03/26/us-nuclear-summit-idUSBRE82P01620120326.* Also see Dan Lamothe, "Russia is greatest threat to the U.S., says Joint Chiefs chairman nominee Gen. Joseph Dunford," *Washington Post,* July 9, 2015, available from *http://www.washingtonpost.com/news/checkpoint/wp/2015/07/09/russia-is-greatest-threat-*

the others; fail to neutralize Moscow, and you are unlikely ever to prevail.[53]

But is this true? Russian President Vladimir Putin has yet to explicitly threaten to destroy the United States.[54] North Korea, however, has.[55] If North Korea followed through with its military threats against South Korea or Japan (two states the United States is bound by formal security agreements to defend), would that not threaten a general war that the United States would be loath to wage? What if Iran acquired nuclear weapons and deployed them to deter the

---

*to-the-u-s-says-joint-chiefs-chairman-nominee-gen-joseph-dunford/*.

53. See e.g., Loren Thompson, "Why Putin's Russia is the Biggest Threat to America in 2015," *Forbes*, January 1, 2015, available from *http://www.forbes.com/sites/lorenthompson/2015/01/02/why-putins-russia-is-the-biggest-threat-to-america-in-2015/* and J.D. Leipold, "Milley: Russia No. 1 Threat to US," *WWW.ARMY.MIL: The Official Homepage of the United States Army*, November 9, 2015, available from *http://www.army.mil/article/158386/Milley__Russia_No_1_threat_to_US/*.

54. Putin, in fact, recently denied that he had any desire to enter in to a nuclear arms race with the United States. See Roland Oliphant, "Vladimir Putin says Russia 'won't start an arms race' at annual press conference that lasts almost four hours," *The Telegraph*, December 23, 2016, available from *http://www.telegraph.co.uk/news/2016/12/23/vladimir-putin-updates-russia-world-annual-press-conference/*. Putin, however, has voiced concerns that the United States may be threatening to destroy Russia. See Katie Mansfield, "US Nuclear War Fears: Vladimir Putin Warns Americans are in 'Impending and Grave Danger,'" *Express*, October 18, 2016, available from *http://www.express.co.uk/news/world/722203/US-Russia-Putin-WW3-nuclear-war-vladimir-putin* and Anna Nemtsova, "Russia Is Building Fallout Shelters to Prepare for a Potential Nuclear Strike," *The Daily Beast*, October 17, 2016, available from *http://www.thedailybeast.com/articles/2016/10/17/russia-is-building-fallout-shelters-to-prepare-for-a-potential-nuclear-strike.html*.

55. See "North Korea threatens to launch nuclear strike on America if it feels threatened and confirms it has a 'first use' preemptive policy," *Daily Mail.com*, October 16, 2016, available from *http://www.dailymail.co.uk/news/article-3842604/It-s-policy-nuclear-North-Korea-says-launch-preemptive-strike-against-threatened.html#ixzz4VtSXivht*.

United States and its Gulf allies from countering Iranian conventional military aggression and covert actions against its neighbors? Such nonnuclear aggression could drive the international price of oil to levels that could strategically weaken both the United States' and most of the world's economies. Would nuclear strategic superiority over Russia enable Washington to counter such concerns?

This set of questions brings us to the views of our academic skeptics. As already noted, this school is split into two groups. The first includes those who think that the further proliferation of nuclear weapons may be beneficial, that upon a state's acquisition of nuclear arms effective nuclear deterrence is automatically assured. The second includes those who question the deterrence value of nuclear arms but who also believe that preventing their proliferation is generally unnecessary or misguided.

What is appealing about the second group is its willingness to take on those who extol the virtues of nuclear deterrence. Did nuclear weapons force Japan to surrender in WWII? *No,* Japan's Emperor only argued they did to save face in surrendering because he knew Japan was destined for defeat by American and Soviet conventional arms. Did they deter the Soviet Union from invading Europe during the Cold War? *No,* what kept the peace after 1945 was the creation of effective East-West security alliance systems and the very real fears these military alliances fostered of a massive, conventional WWIII if Cold War diplomacy failed.

This second group of academics also offers thoughtful rejoinders to the conventional wisdom that nuclear terrorism should be worry number one. Is the threat of nuclear terrorism the most imminent and extreme security threat we face? *Not really.* There are good reasons why no acts of nuclear terrorism have yet taken place and these are likely to apply well into the future. Building or stealing nuclear weapons is too large and complex an operation for most terrorist organizations. A terrorist team tasked to build or seize such weapons would have to worry about being penetrated and betrayed to authorities. Certainly, the high levels of trust and cooperation needed to pull off such efforts would be difficult to maintain. Nor is it in the interest of states that possess such weapons to let anyone but the most trusted and loyal gain access to them.[56]

This pushback to what are now the most popular views on nuclear deterrence and terrorism is edifying. Yet, ultimately one counterfactual on what might have prevented an event (e.g., various post-WWII wars) can hardly trump another. Nor do negative projections on nuclear terrorism top positive ones if only because the future probability of events that have not yet occurred can't be known statistically. In the end, all such projections are speculative.

Moreover, what the two skeptical academic camps agree on—that the dangers associated with nuclear weapons proliferation are exaggerated—is rebuttable. First, they gloss over the serious military risks faced by nations acquiring nuclear weapons. One can see this most clearly by their inattention to the numerous historical cases of preventive military actions taken against states attempting to build their first bomb and to serious plans countries have made to knock out the nuclear capabilities of new nuclear weapons states.

In the first category are the British campaign against the Nazi-operated heavy water plant in Norway, Iran's air strike against Iraq's Osirak reactor in 1980, Israel's attack of the same reactor in 1981, Iraq's repeated strikes against Bushehr between 1984 and 1988,

---

56. See, e.g., John Mueller, "The Atomic Terrorist: Assessing the Likelihood," paper prepared for the Program on International Security Policy, University of Chicago, January 15, 2008, available from *http://politicalscience.osu.edu/faculty/jmueller//apsachgo.pdf* and *Atomic Obsession,* pp. 181-215. Also see Francis J. Gavin, "Same As It Ever Was: Nuclear Alarmism, Proliferation, and the Cold War," *International Security,* Winter 2009/10, pp. 19-23, available from *http://belfercenter.ksg.harvard.edu/files/Gavin.pdf* and Lieber and Press, "Why States Won't Give Nuclear Weapons to Terrorists."

America's air strike against Iraq's nuclear facilities in 1991, Saddam's failed Scud missile strike against Israel's Dimona reactor in the same year, an American Tomahawk strike against Iraq's uranium enrichment plant at Zaafaraniyah, British and American strikes against a variety of suspect Iraqi nuclear sites in 1998, Israel's air strike against Syria's covert nuclear reactor in 2007, and U.S. and Israeli covert and cyber attacks against Iran's nuclear program from 2006 to 2010.

Just as numerous are the occasions that states planned or prepared to knock out the nuclear weapons capabilities of their adversaries. The U.S. military gave serious thought to using nuclear weapons to destroy the Soviet Union's nuclear complex in 1949 and China's in 1964. It also made preliminary military preparations for attacking North Korea's nuclear complex in 1994. The Russians, meanwhile, considered attacking South African nuclear facilities in 1976 after detecting South African preparations to test. They even asked the United States for assistance in making the strike. In 1969, a major border dispute between China and Russia went hot and Moscow gave serious consideration to attacking China's nuclear complex. Two years before, Egypt threatened Israel's production reactor at Dimona. Israel and India, meanwhile, cooperated in several schemes in the 1980s (one of which nearly was implemented) to knock out Pakistan's nuclear weapons facilities at Kahuta.[57]

Second, while most academic skeptics believe nuclear weapons automatically deter aggression nearly perfectly even in small numbers, yet others believe nuclear weapons are militarily useless

---

57. See Fuhrmann, "Preventive War and the Spread of Nuclear Programs;" Isabella Ginor and Gideon Remez, *Foxbats Over Dimona: The Soviets' Nuclear Gamble in the Six-Day War*, New Haven, CT: Yale University Press, 2008 and Tom Cooper, "Joyriding Egyptian Pilots Helped to Provoke the Six-Day War With Israel," *War Is Boring*, October 17, 2016, available from *https://warisboring.com/joyriding-egyptian-pilots-helped-to-provoke-the-six-day-war-with-israel-c2db466aa48d?mc_cid=88408123c2#.3hty6rwjy*.

even if these weapons are numerous and advanced. Because of this, academic skeptics pay little attention to the security risks that may come with deep nuclear weapons reductions—i.e., the transitions from nuclear plenty to zero—risks which are potentially serious.

Finally, academic skeptics tend to ignore or gloss over the risks "upward" nuclear transitions present. These dangers are three-fold. First, as the number of nuclear weapons players increases, the gravity, complexity, and likelihood of ruinous nuclear incidents may increase within states (e.g., unauthorized or accidental use, terrorist theft, irredentist seizure, etc.) and between them (e.g., catalytic wars, misread nuclear signaling, etc.). Second, and closely related, are the numerous technical and managerial challenges each nuclear state faces to make their nuclear forces robust and survivable enough to have any hope of effectively deterring attacks. These challenges are most severe for new nuclear weapons forces but are hardly inconsequential for large, mature forces.[58] Last, as the number of states possessing nuclear forces increases to include nations covered by nuclear security alliance guarantees, the continued viability and coherence of these alliance systems are likely to be tested in the extreme, increasing the prospects for war.[59]

---

58. For the earliest and most accessible discussion of these technical hurdles, see Albert Wohlstetter, "The 'Delicate' Balance of Terror," RAND Paper P-1472, RAND Corporation, Santa Monica, CA, November 6, 1958, available from *http://www.rand.org/about/history/wohlstetter/P1472/P1472.html*. It should be noted that Wohlstetter goes to considerable lengths in his study to spotlight how mastering the technical requirements for securing an effective nuclear deterrent force is essential to prevent preemptive, accidental, and unauthorized nuclear wars as well as nuclear accidents generally. This suggests that attention to these requirements is desirable whatever the merits of nuclear deterrence might be.

59. See note 24; Robert Zarate, "America's Allies and Nuclear Arms: Assessing the Geopolitics of Nonproliferation in Asia," Project 2049 Futuregram 14-002, Project 2049 Institute, Arlington, VA, May 6, 2014, available from *http://www.project2049.net/documents/Zarate_America_Allies_and_Nuclear_Arms_Geopolitics_Nonproliferation*; and Albert Wohlstetter, "Nuclear Sharing and the N + 1 Country," *Foreign Affairs* 39, no. 3, April 1961, pp. 355-387, available from

## *Optimists All*

Putting aside the close calls during the various Cold War crises (e.g., the Cuban Missile Crisis and the possibility of the United States offering France nuclear weapons to use in Vietnam), the nuclear brinkmanship that has been conducted by India and Pakistan, and the nuclear preemption and dares of the Israeli wars of 1967 and 1973,[60] none of the cases noted above seem to support the idea that nuclear proliferation is "inconsequential," much less stabilizing. Just the opposite. Of course, until and unless there is nuclear use, there is no proof in these matters: We can't predict the future with much certainty and the causes of wars are always complex. All we know is that the United States fired nuclear weapons in anger on Hiroshima and Nagasaki, that the United States and Russia threatened to use them several times during the Cold War, but that, for some reason, since 1945, they never have been used.

It would be nice to believe that they never will. Unfortunately, they might. Russia, Pakistan, and North Korea are quite explicit about the advantages of using nuclear weapons first against their adversaries.[61] Some analysts also now believe China's no first use poli-

---

*http://npolicy.org/userfiles/file/Nuclear%20Heuristics-Nuclear%20Sharing.pdf.*

60. See Logevall, "'We Might Give Them a Few;" Peter Lavoy, "Islamabad's Nuclear Posture: Its Premises and Implementation," in Henry Sokolski, ed., *Pakistan's Nuclear Future: Worries beyond War*, Carlisle, PA: Strategic Studies Institute, U.S. Army War College, 2008, pp. 129-166, available from *http://npolicy.org/books/Pakistans_Nuclear_Worries/Ch5_Lavoy.pdf*; and Ori Rabinowitz, *Bargaining on Nuclear Tests: Washington and Its Cold War Deals*, Oxford: Oxford University Press, 2014, pp. 70-105.

61. See Yury E. Fedorov, "Russia's Nuclear Policy," a paper presented before the National Institute for Defense Studies 12th International Symposium on Security Affairs, "Major Powers' Nuclear Policies and International Order in the 21st Century," Tokyo, November 18, 2009, available from *http://www.nids.go.jp/english/event/symposium/pdf/2009/e_04.pdf*; Mark Schneider, *The Nuclear Forces and Doctrine of the Russian Federation*, Fairfax, VA: National Institute

cies may be undergoing revision.[62] All of these states, plus Israel, North Korea, and India are increasing or modernizing their nuclear arsenals. If these states are followed by Iran, South Korea, Japan, Turkey, the United Arab Emirates (UAE), or Saudi Arabia,[63] the chances for nuclear miscalculations and war would likely go up, not down.[64]

---

Press, 2006, available from *http://www.nipp.org/wp-content/uploads/2014/12/ China-nuclear-final-pub.pdf*; "Russia carried out practice nuclear strike against Sweden," *The Local*, February 3, 2016, available from *http://www.thelocal. se/20160203/russia-did-practice-a-nuclear-strike-against-sweden*; Commander Muhammad Azam Khan, "India's Cold Start Is Too Hot," *U.S. Naval Institute Proceedings* 137, no. 3, March 2011, available from *www.usni.org/magazines/ proceedings/2011-03/indias-cold-start-too-hot*; Henry Sokolski, ed., *Pakistan's Nuclear Future: Worries beyond War,* Carlisle, PA: Strategic Studies Institute, U.S. Army War College, 2008, pp. 129-166, available from *http://npolicy.org/ thebook.php?bid=6*; and Dana Ford, "North Korea threatens nuclear strike over U.S.-South Korean exercises," *CNN*, March 7, 2016, available from *http://www. cnn.com/2016/03/06/asia/north-korea-preemptive-nuclear-strike-threat/*.

62. See William R. Hawkins, "Nuclear Warfare Is Still Possible," *Fortuna's Corner* (blog), June 5, 2014, available from *http://fortunascorner.com/2014/06/07/ nuclear-warfare-is-still-possible/comment-page-1/*; John Chan, "Chinese Security Analyst Questions 'No First Use' Nuclear Policy," *World Socialist Watch*, August 15, 2013, available from *http://www.wsws.org/en/articles/2013/08/15/nuke-a15. html*; Michael Mazza and Dan Blumenthal, "China's Strategic Forces in the 21st Century: The People's Liberation Army's Changing Nuclear Doctrine and Force Posture," in Henry D. Sokolski, ed. *The Next Arms Race,* Carlisle, PA: Strategic Studies Institute, 2012, pp. 83-111, available from *http://npolicy.org/books/Next_ Arms_Race/Ch3_Mazza-Blumenthal.pdf*; and Stephanie Spies, "China's Nuclear Policy: (No) First Use?" *PONI Debates the Issues* (blog), October 20, 2011, available from *http://poniforum.csis.org/blog/poni-debates-the-issues-u-s-no-first-use*.

63. See Kidd, "Nuclear Proliferation Risk - Is It Vastly Overrated?" Kidd, a nuclear power proponent who subscribes to the optimistic view of the nuclear neorealist skeptics, projects that there will "only" be roughly six more nuclear-armed states by 2030. He did not name them and it is impossible to know which states might go nuclear next, but the six listed here are among the most frequently mentioned in the current literature.

64. See Thomas W. Graham, "Nuclear Weapons Stability or Anarchy in the 21st

Again, it may well be, as one recent analysis suggested, that the prospects for war will decline as soon as there is "symmetry" between any two nuclear states. This conclusion, however, begs the question of precisely when and how such "symmetry" might be achieved or perceived by each party. This matters since this same analysis concludes that without such nuclear symmetry, the prospects for conflict are increased.[65]

Nor can we assume that the consequences of nuclear use will be minor. Total industrial wars may no longer be likely. But, this hardly precludes the possibility of "limited" nuclear conflicts.[66] Also, with advanced societies' newfound distaste for protracted wars has come an increased intolerance for violence. America's security state reaction to 9/11 certainly suggests the public desire for security has reached a new all-time high. A nuclear event almost anywhere, as a result, is likely to prompt even more security (i.e., repressive) governance. Think *Nineteen Eighty-Four*. For governments originally dedicated to the proposition of enlightened self-

---

Century: China, India, and Pakistan," in *The Next Arms Race*, pp. 262-304, available from *http://npolicy.org/books/Next_Arms_Race/Ch9_Graham.pdf.*

65. See Cf. Robert Rauchhaus, "Evaluating the Nuclear Peace Hypothesis: A Quantitative Approach," *Journal of Conflict Resolution* 53, no. 2, April 2009, pp. 258-277 and Erik Gartzke, "Nuclear Proliferation Dynamics and Conventional Conflict," a paper originally presented at the 50th Annual Convention of the International Studies Association, New York, February 15-18, 2009, available from *http://pages.ucsd.edu/~egartzke/papers/nuketime_05032010.pdf.*

66. See Sydney J. Freedberg Jr., "No Longer Unthinkable: Should U.S. Ready for 'Limited' Nuclear War?" *Breaking Defense*, May 30, 2013, available from *http://breakingdefense.com/2013/05/no-longer-unthinkable-should-us-ready-for-limited-nuclear-war/* and Arms Control Association, "Russia's Military Doctrine," *Arms Control Today*, May 1, 2000, available from *http://www.armscontrol.org/act/2000_05/dc3ma00.*

rule, this should be a concern.[67] At the very least, it ought to inform our thinking about nuclear weapons and their possible use.

Yet, those eager to go to zero ultimately do not appear to be all that worried that states might intentionally use these weapons. Just the opposite. Most nuclear abolitionists allow that nuclear weapons are only useful to deter nuclear attacks and believe that they do. For them, it would be irrational for states to use nuclear weapons to secure military advantage. Nor do they seriously consider that Russia, Pakistan, North Korea, or China might be developing their nuclear forces for purposes other than deterrence. Their worries instead focus optimistically on the yet unrealized threats of nuclear terrorism, accidental detonations, and unauthorized use. Finally, they're convinced that deeper U.S. nuclear reductions will prompt others to follow suit and insist that despite the not so peaceful past nuclear activities of India, Iraq, Iran, Egypt, Turkey, North Korea, South Korea, Taiwan, and Syria, sharing more dual-use nuclear technology will help strengthen the NPT.

---

67. See E. U. Condon; "The New Technique of Private War," in Dexter Masters and Katherine Way, editors, *One World or None,* Washington, DC: Federation of American Scientists, 2007, pp. 107-15; Russell Hardin, "Civil Liberties in the Era of Mass Terror," *Journal of Ethics* 8, no. 1, March 2004, pp. 77-95, available from *http://www.nyu.edu/gsas/dept/politics/faculty/hardin/research/CivLiberties.pdf*; David Bartoshuk, John Diamond, and Peter Heussy, "Nuclear Terrorism: Local Effects, Global Consequences," Saga Foundation, July 2008, available from *http://www.sagafoundation.org/SagaFoundationWhitePaperSAGAMARK7282008.pdf*; James D. Fearon, "Catastrophic Terrorism and Civil Liberties in the Short and Long Run," paper prepared for the symposium on "Constitutions, Democracy, and the Rule of Law," Columbia University, New York, October 17, 2003, available from *https://www.stanford.edu/group/fearon-research/cgi-bin/wordpress/wp-content/uploads/2013/10/Catastrophic-terrorism-and-civil-liberties-in-the-short-and-long-run.pdf*; and Matthew Fuhrmann, "After Armageddon: The Potential Political Consequences of the Third Use of Nuclear Weapons," in Henry Sokolski, ed., *Should We Let the Bomb Spread?* Carlisle, PA: Strategic Studies Institute, 2016, pp. 183-212, available from *http://www.strategicstudiesinstitute.army.mil/pubs/display.cfm?pubID=1327*.

Nuclear hawks, meanwhile, may fear that our enemies might use nuclear weapons but are cautiously optimistic that the United States and its allies can be made safe against such threats so long as the right number of nuclear weapons of the right kind in the right hands are on the ready and the United States and its friends are willing and able to knockout proliferators' nuclear projects in a timely fashion through conventional military strikes and covert action. Regarding the nuclear security concerns of the abolitionists, they are similarly upbeat: We have avoided accidental and illicit use so far; with due diligence we can manage this problem into the future.

Finally, academic skeptics are perhaps the most optimistic of all: Further nuclear proliferation is either good or, at least, not a worry. Nuclear weapons deter nuclear wars completely or are so useless they never will be used.

Each of our current views of nuclear proliferation, then, ends up serving our highest hopes. The question is: Do they adequately address what we should be most worried about? Do they deal with the possible military diversion of "peaceful" nuclear energy—a dual-use technology likely to spread further? Do they adequately address the perils of making nuclear cuts as other states continue to maintain or increase their arsenals? Do they assume that if we maintain our nuclear weapons force capabilities, we will forever deter the worst? Do they fully consider the military risks states run when they acquire their first nuclear weapon or try to ramp up existing arsenals significantly? Can any of them by themselves serve as a practical guide to reduce the nuclear challenges we face?

# WHERE WE ARE HEADED

With most of the world's advanced economies still stuttering in recession or in slow growth, Western support for increased defense spending low or uncertain,[68] and a major emerging Asian power increasingly at military odds with its neighbors and the United States, it is tempting to view our times as rhyming with a decade of similar woes—the disorderly 1930s.[69]

---

68. See Pew Research Center, "Public Uncertain, Divided Over America's Place in the World," *U.S. Politics and Policy*, May 5, 2016, available from *http://www. people-press.org/2016/05/05/public-uncertain-divided-over-americas-place-in-the-world/* and Bruce Stokes, Richard Wike, and Jacob Poushter,"Europeans Wary of Hard Power," *Global Attitudes and Trends*, June 2016, available from *http://www.pewglobal.org/2016/06/13/europeans-wary-of-hard-power/*.

69. See, e.g., Matthew Continetti, "A World in Crisis: What the Thirties Tell Us about Today," *Weekly Standard*, January 3, 2011, available from *http://www. weeklystandard.com/articles/world-crisis_524865.html*; "Briefing—Lessons of the 1930s: There Could Be Trouble Ahead," *The Economist*, December 10, 2011, pp. 76-78; Joe Weisenthal, "Tim Geithner Warns: The U.S. at Risk of a 1930s Repeat," *Business Insider*, September 12, 2010, available from *http://www. businessinsider.com/geithner-the-us-is-at-risk-of-a-repeat-of-the-1930s-2010-9*; Thomas Walkom, "Eurozone Crisis Signals a Repeat of the 1930s Crisis," *Star* (Toronto), May 13, 2014, available from *http://www.thestar.com/news/canada/2012/05/15/walkom_eurozone_crisis_signals_a_repeat_of_the_1930s. html*; and Roger Cohen, "Yes, It Could Happen Again," *Atlantic*, July 29, 2014,

Might we again be drifting toward some new form of mortal national combat? Or, will our future more likely ape the near-half-century that defined the Cold War—a period in which tensions between competing states ebbed and flowed but peace mostly prevailed by dint of nuclear mutual fear and loathing?

The short answer is, nobody knows. This much, however, is clear: The strategic military competitions of the next two decades will be unlike any the world has yet seen. Assuming U.S., Chinese, Russian, Israeli, Indian, French, British, Pakistani, and North Korean strategic forces continue to be modernized and America and Russia freeze or further reduce their strategic nuclear deployments, the next arms race will be run by a much larger number of contestants with highly destructive strategic capabilities far more closely matched and capable of being quickly enlarged than in any other previous period in history.

## *Looking Backward*

To grasp the dimensions of this brave new world, one need only compare how capable states were of striking their adversaries suddenly a half-century ago, with what damage they might inflict today. In 1962, Washington and Moscow engaged in the most significant of Cold War nuclear confrontations over the Soviet deployment of nuclear-capable missiles in Cuba. At the time, the United States had over 24,000 operationally deployed nuclear weapons. Russia had nearly 2,500. The other nuclear powers—the UK and France—had an aggregate of no more than 50 (with

---

available from *http://www.theatlantic.com/magazine/archive/2014/08/yes-it-could-happen-again/373465/*. There are, of course, other views. See, e.g., Kishore Mahbubani and Lawerence Summers, "The Fusion of Civilizations: The Case for Global Optimism," *Foreign Affairs*, June 12, 2016, available from *https://www.foreignaffairs.com/articles/2016-04-18/fusion-civilizations*.

France possessing few, if any, deployed nuclear weapons).[70] The difference in nuclear weapons deployment numbers between the top and bottom nuclear powers—a figure equal to at least three orders of magnitude—was massive. America, moreover, was clearly dominant.

In contrast, today, the United States has slightly less than 2,000 deployed strategic and tactical nuclear warheads and Russia roughly 3,500.[71] India, Pakistan, the UK, France, and Israel have 100 to 400 each, and China may have anywhere from between 190

---

70. See Natural Resources Defense Council, "Table of Global Nuclear Weapons Stockpiles, 1945-2002."

71. As of late 2016, the official number of deployed strategic warheads as counted under the New START Treaty (which count heavy bombers as one warhead) places the number of U.S. warheads at 1,367 and Russia at 1,796. See U.S. Department of State, "New START Treaty Aggregate Numbers of Strategic Offensive Arms," October 1, 2016, available from *https://web.archive.org/web/20161010084018/ http://m.state.gov/md262624.htm*. Other sources count more than one warhead per bomber. An average of their estimates places the number of U.S. deployed strategic warheads at 1,750, plus 180 tactical warheads deployed in Europe for a total of 1,930 deployed warheads. The average estimate of Russian deployed strategic warheads is 1,800. Russia is also estimated to have around 2,000 tactical warheads that the Russian government says are in central storage, which brings the total of Russian warheads to 3,800. The figures for each country do not include warheads considered to be nondeployed or awaiting dismantlement. See Hans M. Kristensen and Robert S. Norris, "United States Nuclear Forces, 2016" *Bulletin of the Atomic Scientists* 72, no. 2, March 2016, pp. 63-73, available from *http://www.tandfonline.com/doi/pdf/10.1080/00963402.2016.1145901*; Hans M. Kristensen, "Tac Nuke Numbers Confirmed?" *FAS Strategic Security Blog*, Federation of American Scientists, December 7, 2010, available from *http://fas.org/blogs/security/2010/12/tacnukes/*; Hans M. Kristensen and Robert S. Norris, "Russian Nuclear Forces, 2016" *Bulletin of the Atomic Scientists* 72, no. 3, March/ April 2016, pp. 125-134, available from *http://www.tandfonline.com/doi/pdf/10.1080/0 0963402.2016.1170359*; Hans M. Kristensen, "Status of World Nuclear Forces," *Federation of American Scientists*, updated May 26, 2016, available from *https:// fas.org/issues/nuclear-weapons/status-world-nuclear-forces/*; and Shannon Kile and Hans Kristensen, "Trends in World Nuclear Forces, 2016," *Stockholm International Peace Research Institute*, June 2016, available from *https://www.sipri.org/sites/default/files/FS%201606%20WNF_Embargo_Final%20A.pdf*.

to 900.[72] Putting aside North Korea's nascent nuclear force (cf. France's force of 1962), the difference in the numbers of nuclear deployments between the top and bottom nuclear powers, then, has fallen at least two full orders of magnitude and is projected to decline even further (see Figure 2 on the next page).

---

72. The UK has 120 deployed warheads and France has 280 deployed warheads. India, Pakistan, Israel and China do not distinguish between deployed and stored warheads. See "Nuclear Weapons: Who Has What at a Glance," *Arms Control Association,* updated October 2016, available from *https://www.armscontrol. org/factsheets/Nuclearweaponswhohaswhat*; Kristensen, "Status of World Nuclear Forces"; Hans M. Kristensen and Robert S. Norris, "Global nuclear weapons inventories, 1945-2013"; Shannon N. Kile and Hans M. Kristensen, "World Nuclear Forces," *SIPRI Yearbook 2013: Armaments, Disarmament and International Security,* Oxford: Oxford University Press, 2013, overview available from *http://web.archive.org/web/20130812064732/http://www.sipri. org/yearbook/2013/files/sipri-yearbook-2013-chapter-6-overview*; and Timothy McDonnell, "Nuclear Pursuits: Non-P-5 nuclear-armed states, 2013," *Bulletin of the Atomic Scientists* 69, no. 1, January/February 2013, pp. 62-70, available from *http://bos.sagepub.com/content/69/1/62.full*. For the UK, also see "Country Profile: United Kingdom," *Nuclear Threat Initiative*, updated July 2014, available from *http://www.nti.org/country-profiles/united-kingdom/*. For Pakistan, also see Hans M. Kristensen and Robert S. Norris, "Pakistani Nuclear Forces, 2015," *Bulletin of the Atomic Scientists*, October 19, 2015, available from *http://bos. sagepub.com/content/early/2015/10/06/0096340215611090.full*. For Israel, also see Warner D. Farr, "The Third Temple's Holy of Holies: Israel's Nuclear Weapons," *Counterproliferation Paper No. 2,* USAF Counterproliferation Center, Maxwell Air Force Base, AL, September 1999, available from *http://www.au.af.mil/au/awc/awcgate/cpc-pubs/farr.htm*. For China, also see Hans M. Kristensen and Robert S. Norris, "Chinese Nuclear Forces, 2013," *Bulletin of the Atomic Scientists* 69, no. 6, November/December 2013, pp. 79-86, available from *http://bos.sagepub.com/content/69/6/79.full*; Bill Gertz, "The Warhead Gap," *Washington Free Beacon*, November 9, 2012, available from *http:// freebeacon.com/national-security/the-warhead-gap/*; and "Nuclear Weapons: China's Nuclear Forces," *GlobalSecurity.org,* July 7, 2014, available from *http:// www.globalsecurity.org/wmd/world/china/nuke.htm*.

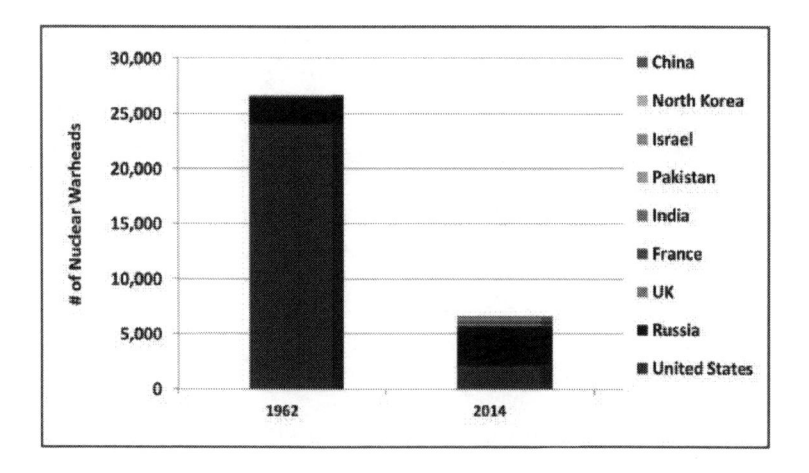

**Figure 2: From U.S. Strategic Dominance to a Compressed Nuclear Crowd.**[73]

As tight as the nuclear deployments between the world's nuclear-armed states has become, the potential for this nuclear balance to shift quickly and dramatically is far greater than it was a half-century ago. In 1962, the United States, Russia, the UK, and France had militarized nearly all of the nuclear weapons materials they had. They held little or nothing back in reserve. Nor could any of them militarize significant civilian stockpiles of separated plutonium or highly-enriched uranium (HEU), as no such stockpiles were then available.

---

73. The information used to generate this graph was drawn from the sources in notes 70-72. Data for North Korea's arsenal was drawn from David Albright and Christina Walrond, "North Korea's Estimated Stocks of Plutonium and Weapons Grade Uranium," *Institute for Science and International Security*, August 16, 2012, available from *http://isis-online.org/uploads/isis-reports/documents/dprk_fissile_material_production_16Aug2012.pdf* and Siegfried S. Hecker, "Lessons learned from the North Korean nuclear crises," *Daedalus*, Winter 2010, pp. 44-56, available from *http://cisac.fsi.stanford.edu/sites/default/files/evnts/media/HeckerDaedalusDPRK.pdf*. In the case of the United States, Russia, UK, and France, only deployed warheads are shown. For all other countries, both deployed and stored warheads are shown.

Today, things are different. First, the United States and Russia alone can redeploy thousands of reserve nuclear weapons and reconfigure stockpiled fissile materials into tens of thousands of additional nuclear weapons. Second, officials in Japan have publicly allowed they have the means to militarize nearly 11 metric tons of civilian plutonium (i.e., enough to make more than 2,000 first-generation bombs)[74] material domestically.[75]

---

74. The number of kilograms of weapons-grade plutonium required to make a first-generation Nakagaski bomb is set in this book conservatively at four kilograms—the number the U.S. Department of Energy (DoE) has used. See "DPRK: Plutonium Program," *GlobalSecurity.org*, available from *http://www.globalsecurity.org/wmd/world/dprk/nuke-plutonium.htm* and "Nuclear Weapon Design," Federation of American Scientists, October 21, 1998, available from *http://fas.org/nuke/intro/nuke/design.htm*. The actual figure needed to fuel any given bomb may be more or less, depending on how advanced the weapons design is. The Soviet Union, for example, tested a device in 1953 that used only 2 kilograms of plutonium. That weapon produced a yield of 5.8 kilotons. It also tested a weapon in 1953 that used only 0.8 kilograms of plutonium. It produced a yield of 1.6 kilotons. See Pavel Podvig, "Amounts of Fissile Materials in Early Soviet Nuclear Devices," *International Panel on Fissile Materials Blog*, October 1, 2012, available from *http://fissilematerials.org/blog/2012/10/amounts_of_fissile_materi.html* and Thomas B. Cochran and Christopher E. Paine, "The Amount of Plutonium and Highly-Enriched Uranium Needed for Pure Fission Nuclear Weapons" working paper, Washington, DC, Natural Resources Defense Council, April 13, 1998, available from *http://www.nrdc.org/nuclear/fissionw/fissionweapons.pdf*. The amount of reactor-grade plutonium required to make a first-generation Nagasaki bomb is set in this book at 5.2 kilograms, or 30 percent more than the official DoE figure for weapons-grade plutonium. See Richard L. Garwin, "Reactor-Grade Plutonium Can be Used to Make Powerful and Reliable Nuclear Weapons: Separated Plutonium in the Fuel Cycle Must Be Protected as If It Were Nuclear Weapons," August 26, 1998, available from *http://fas.org/rlg/980826-pu.htm*.

75. See Katsuhisa Furukawa, "Nuclear Option, Arms Control, and Extended Deterrence: In Search of a New Framework for Japan's Nuclear Policy," in Benjamin L. Self and Jeffrey W. Thompson eds., *Japan's Nuclear Option: Security, Politics, and Policy in the 21st Century*, Washington, DC: Stimson Center, 2003, pp. 95-147, available from *http://www.stimson.org/images/uploads/research-pdfs/56Policy_Context.pdf*; Frank Von Hippel, "Plutonium, Proliferation and Radioactive-Waste Politics in East Asia," in *The Next Arms*

India, meanwhile, has many hundreds of bombs' worth of separated reactor-grade plutonium on tap, is planning to expand its capacity to produce more of this material significantly over the next 3 to 10 years, and has claimed to have tested a nuclear device using this reactor-grade material.[76] Third, China has produced tons of nuclear material that it might yet militarize and is considering building a civilian plutonium reprocessing plant that could produce over 1,500 bombs' worth of plutonium annually.[77]

---

*Race*, pp. 111-140, available from *http://npolicy.org/books/Next_Arms_Race/ Ch4_vonHippel.pdf*; Takuya Suzuki, "Nuclear Leverage: Long an Advocate of Nuclear Energy, Nakasone Now Says Japan Should Go Solar," *Asahi Shimbun*, July 7, 2011, available from *http://ajw.asahi.com/article/0311disaster/analysis_ opinion/AJ201107214814*; Douglas Birch and R. Jeffrey Smith, "Plutonium Fever Blossoms in Japan," *Center for Public Integrity*, May 19, 2014, in which Japan's former defense minister in 2012, Satoshi Morimoto, is quoted saying that the country's nuclear power reactors have "very great defensive deterrent functions," available from *http://www.publicintegrity.org/2014/03/12/14394/plutonium-fever-blossoms-Japan*; and a radio interview of former Japanese Prime Minister Naoto Kan noted that having plutonium on hand to have an option to make bombs was one of the reasons why Japan under Nakasone originally backed nuclear power. See "Ex-Japanese PM on How Fukushima Meltdown was Worse Than Chernobyl and Why He Now Opposes Nuclear Power," *Democracy Now*, March 11, 2014, available from *http://www.democracynow.org/2014/3/11/ex_japanese_ pm_on_how_fukushima*.

76. See International Panel on Fissile Materials, *Plutonium Separation in Nuclear Power Programs: Status, Problems, and Prospects of Civilian Reprocessing Around the World*, July 2015, p. 58 ff, available from *http://fissilematerials. org/library/2015/07/plutonium_separation_in_nuclea.html*; Zia Mian, A.H. Nayyar, R. Rajaraman, and M.V. Ramana, "Fissile Materials in South Asia and the Implications of the U.S.-India Nuclear Deal," in Henry D. Sokolski, ed., *Pakistan's Nuclear Future: Worries Beyond War*, 192-195, available from *http:// npolicy.org/books/Pakistans_Nuclear_Worries/Ch6_Mian-Nayyar-Rajaraman-Ramana.pdf*; and Zahir Kazmi, "Normalizing the Non-proliferation Regime," *Survival* 57, no. 1, Feb/March 2015.

77. See World New Association, "China's Nuclear Fuel Cycle," update December 6, 2016, available from *http://www.world-nuclear.org/information-library/ country-profiles/countries-a-f/china-nuclear-fuel-cycle.aspx* and International Panel on Fissile Materials, *Global Fissile Material Report 2015*, p. 31, available

Pakistan, Iran, Israel, South Korea, and North Korea also either make or are planning to produce such nuclear fuels (see Figure 3):

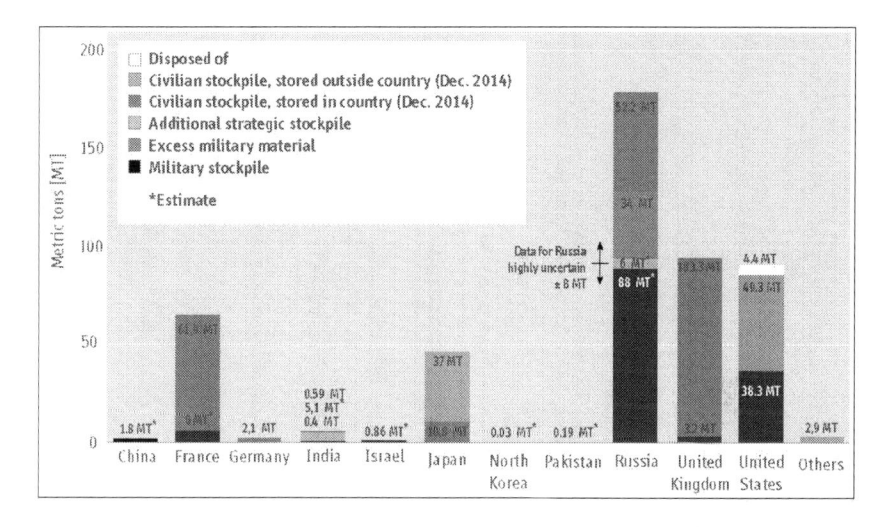

**Figure 3. National Stockpiles of Separated Plutonium.**[78]

As for enriched uranium, the United States and Russia each still easily have more than 10,000 crude bombs' worth of surplus weapons-grade uranium on hand (see Figure 4 on the next page):

---

from *http://fissilematerials.org/library/gfmr15.pdf*.

78. See International Panel on Fissile Materials (IPFM), *Global Fissile Materials Report 2015*, p. 25.

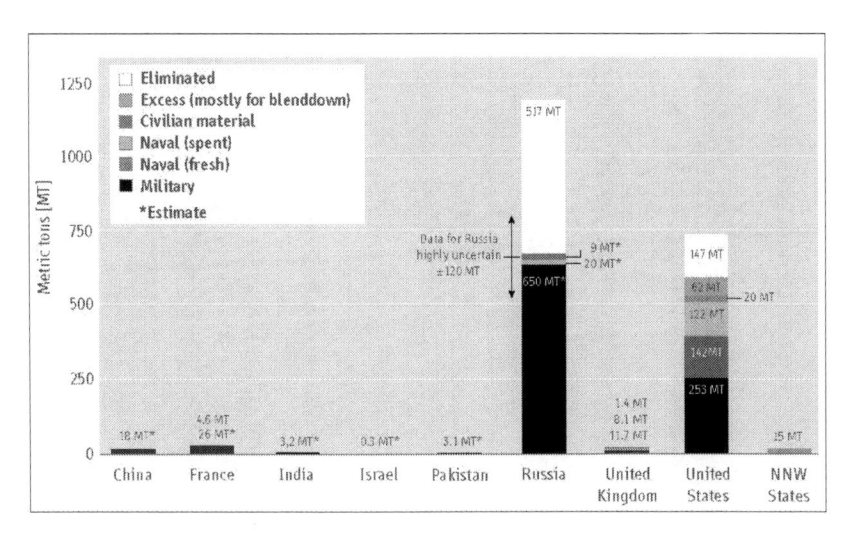

52     *Underestimated: Our Not So Peaceful Nuclear Future*

**Figure 4. National Stockpiles of Highly-Enriched Uranium.**[79]

The amount China may have deployed in weapons is unclear but a conservative estimate of the HEU it has produced is 16 metric tons—i.e., enough to make roughly 800 first-generation implosion weapons.[80] India, meanwhile, has enough highly-enriched uranium

---

79. Ibid, p. 12.

80. A 10-to 20-kiloton yield nuclear weapon would roughly require between 12-20 kilograms of weapons-grade uranium. If the Chinese should choose to use the advanced nuclear weapons designs that they clearly have on hand, the fissile requirements could drop to between 4 to 5 kilograms of weapons-grade uranium per 10-to 20-kiloton yield device. It also should be noted that plutonium can be used with highly enriched uranium in a manner that would significantly reduce the amount of HEU required. Thus, the amount of weapons-grade uranium required for a given critical mass can be reduced by roughly 50 percent simply by using two kilograms of plutonium in the core. On these points and China's estimated HEU holdings, see Cochran and Paine, "The Amount of Plutonium and Highly-Enriched Uranium;" Harold A. Feiveson, Alexander Glaser, Zia Mian and Frank N. von Hippel, *Unmaking the Bomb: A Fissile Material Approach to Nuclear Disarmament and Nonproliferation*, Cambridge, MA: MIT Press, 2014, pp. 38-39 and 54-56; Gregory S. Jones, "An Iran Nuclear Deal That Spreads Nuclear Weapons," August 10, 2015, available from *http://nebula. wsimg.com/de41a0d1cf9f9c51df7637d3b8df3d05?AccessKeyId=40C80D0B514*

stockpiled to make several hundred additional crude nuclear implosion weapons, as do France and the UK (again, see Figure 4). As for the future, both Japan and China plan on expanding their uranium enrichment capacity significantly. South Korea would like to enrich uranium as well. As will be discussed, all of these efforts are likely to be in excess of anything called for commercially.

This, then, brings us to the next qualitative strategic metric of interest, long-range missile delivery systems. In 1962, only the United States and the Soviet Union had missiles capable of delivering a first-generation nuclear weapon any distance. Today, 24 states do.[81] To be sure, many of these states only have theater-range systems. But most of these states are in hotspots like the Middle East, where missiles of such range are more than sufficient to strike several neighbors.[82] Meanwhile, the rest of the world's nuclear-capable missile states can target this same region with intercontinental or medium-range systems.

As for the total number of nuclear-armed states, this figure has increased as well. A half-century ago, only the United States, Russia, the UK, and France had nuclear arms, and an overwhelm-

---

*71CD869 75&disposition=0&alloworigin=1*; and H.C. Paxton, "Los Alamos Critical Mass Data," Los Alamos Scientific Laboratory Report, LA-3067-MS, December 1975, 51, available from *http://www.iaea.org/inis/collection/ NCLCollectionStore/_Public/07/244/7244852.pdf.*

81. See Arms Control Association, "Worldwide Ballistic Missile Inventories," updated July 2014, available from *http://www.armscontrol.org/factsheets/ missiles*; Nuclear Threat Initiative, "Country Profiles," available from *http:// www.nti.org/country-profiles/*; and Missilethreat.com, "Missiles of the World," accessed August 13, 2014, available from *http://missilethreat.com/missiles-of-the-world/.*

82. See Stein, "A Gordian Knot: Missiles in the Gulf," *Arms Control Wonk* (blog), April 30, 2014, available from *http://guests.armscontrolwonk.com/ archive/4372/a-gordian-knot-missiles-in-the-gulf.*

ing number of these weapons were in the hands of the United States (see Figure 5 below):

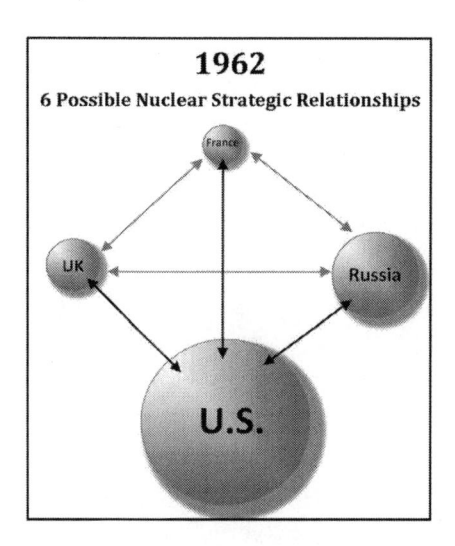

**Figure 5. Four Nuclear Weapons States in 1962.**

Now, there are nine nuclear-armed states. Two—the UK and France—are within NATO and, to a limited extent, coordinate their nuclear weapons efforts.[83] North Korea, meanwhile, is a state that the major powers hope will give up its nuclear arms in negotiations. In this world, U.S. officials like to think that most of the currently nuclear-armed states are either U.S. allies or strategic partners (see Figure 6):

---

83. See, Matthew Harries, "Britain and France As Nuclear Partners," *Survival*, February-March 2012, available from *http://www.iiss.org/en/publications/survival/sections/2012-23ab/survival--global-politics-and-strategy-february-march-2012-7116/54-1-02-harries-9500*.

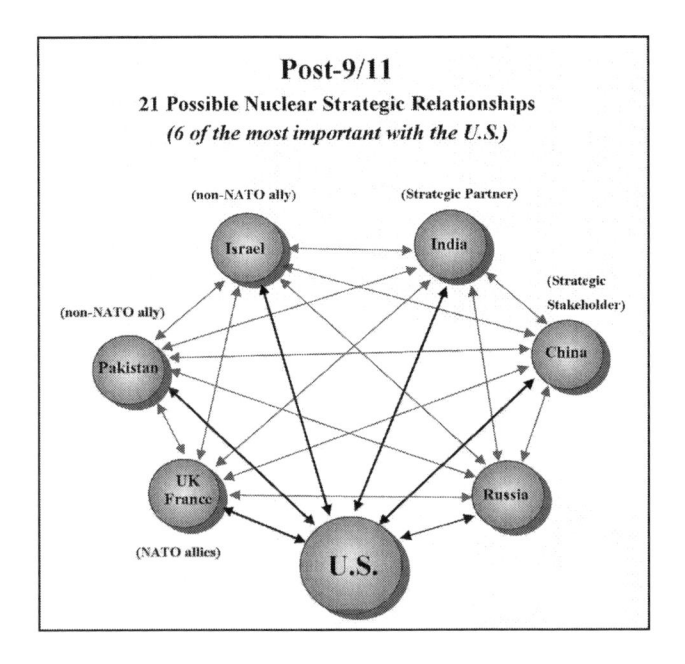

**Figure 6. How the U.S. Views the World Today.**

This world, however, may not last. Certainly, Tehran may yet militarize its nuclear holdings, and Turkey, Saudi Arabia, Algeria, South Korea, and Japan must now all be viewed as possible near or mid-term nuclear weapons-ready states. Also, unlike France, China, Russia, and the UK, these post-Cold War nuclear-weapons aspirants may not announce their acquisition of their first nuclear weapon by testing it. Instead, they are likely to develop "peaceful" nuclear energy programs, as Iran, India, Iraq, and North Korea did, and then move toward nuclear weapons only when they conclude it is useful to do so.

Whether or not "safety" and nuclear stability in this new world will be "the sturdy child of [mutual] terror" (Winston Churchill's description of Cold War stability),[84] remains to be seen. Certainly, the stool of nuclear deterrence will have many more strategic legs that could give way in many more surprising ways than were possible a half century ago (see Figure 7 below):

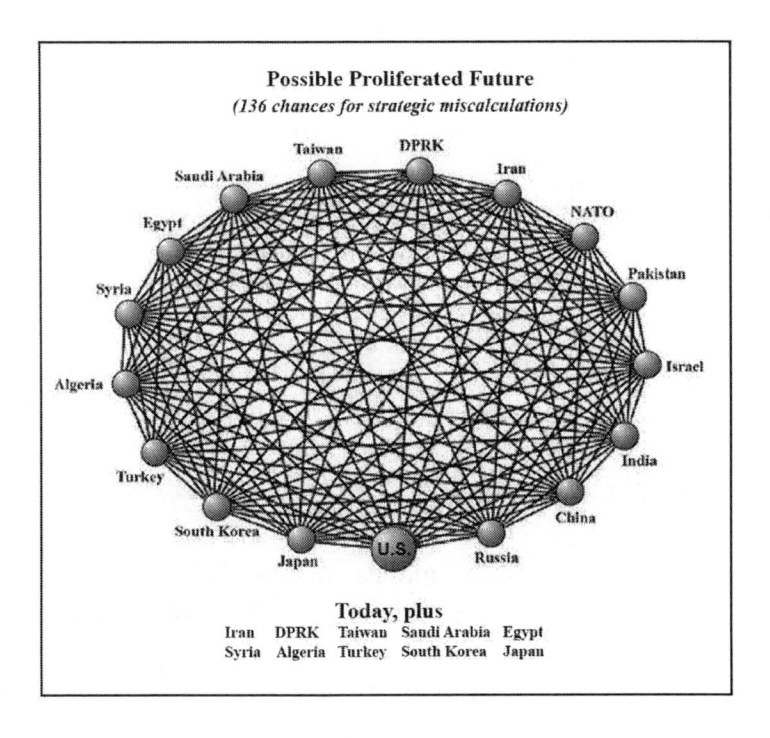

**Possible Proliferated Future**
*(136 chances for strategic miscalculations)*

Taiwan, DPRK, Iran, NATO, Pakistan, Israel, India, China, Russia, U.S., Japan, South Korea, Turkey, Algeria, Syria, Egypt, Saudi Arabia

**Today, plus**
Iran  DPRK  Taiwan  Saudi Arabia  Egypt
Syria  Algeria  Turkey  South Korea  Japan

**Figure 7. Possible Proliferated Future.**

---

84. See Winston Churchill, "Never Despair" (text of speech before the House of Commons, London, March 1, 1955), available from *http://www.winstonchurchill.org/resources/speeches/1946-1963-elder-statesman/102-never-despair*.

## *Why Worry?*

As already noted, a fashionable rejoinder to such broodings is to insist that all of these states will be mutually deterred. Any intelligent state, it is argued, should know that using nuclear weapons is militarily self-defeating and that these weapons' only legitimate mission is to deter military threats. According to this view, fretting about nuclear use and proliferation is mistaken or overwrought.[85]

But is it? Can states deter military threats with nuclear weapons if their actual use is universally viewed as being self-defeating? Which nuclear-armed states, if any, actually believe they are militarily useless? As noted earlier, the Russians and Pakistanis clearly do not. Just the opposite: They have gone out of their way to develop battlefield nuclear weapons and plan to use them first to deter and defeat opposing advanced conventional forces. As for the United States, France, and the UK, all have studiously refused to renounce first use. Israel, meanwhile, insists that while it will not be first to introduce nuclear weapons in the Middle East, it will not be second. This leaves North Korea—a wild card—and India and China, whose declared no first use policies are either unclear or under reconsideration.[86]

---

85. See, e.g., Mueller, *Atomic Obsession*, pp. 129-42; Idem, *Overblown: How Politicians and the Terrorism Industry Inflate National Security Threats and Why We Believe Them,* New York: Free Press, 2006; and Kidd, "Nuclear Proliferation Risk - Is It Vastly Overrated?"

86. See, e.g., notes 61 and 62; Anil A. Anthale, "Why Modi Wants to Change India's Nuclear Policy," *Rediff News*, May 13, 2014, available from *http://www.rediff.com/news/column/ls-election-why-modi-wants-to-change-indias-nuclear-policy/20140513.htm*; P.R. Chari, "India's Nuclear Doctrine: Stirrings of Change," *Carnegie Endowment for International Peace*, June 4, 2014, available from *http://carnegieendowment.org/2014/06/04/india-s-nuclear-doctrine-stirrings-of-change/hcks*; Liping Xia, "China's Nuclear Doctrine: Debates and Evolution," *Regional Voices on the Challenges of Nuclear Deterrence Stability in Southern Asia,* Washington, DC: Carnegie Endowment, June 30, 2016; Fiona

But are not the days of highly destructive wars—nuclear or non-nuclear—behind us? Certainly, with the events surrounding 9/11, this view has gained increasing support from a number of U.S. and allied military analysts and pundits.[87] Reflecting this outlook, the United States and its European allies have turned several Cold War nuclear "survival" bunkers into private real estate offerings or historical tourist sites.[88]

---

S. Cunningham and M. Taylor Fravel, "Assuring Assured Retaliation: China's Nuclear Posture and US-China Strategic Stability," *International Security*, Fall 2015, pp. 7-50; and Hwang Sung-Hee, "N. Korea Leader Orders Nuclear Arsenal on Standby," *Yahoo News*, March 4, 2016, available from *https://www.yahoo.com/news/n-korea-leader-orders-nuclear-arsenal-standby-kcna-223744330.html?ref=gs*.

87. This debate, however, is ongoing. C.f., Graham Allison, "Just How Likely Is Another World War?" *The Atlantic*, July 30, 2014, available from *http://www.theatlantic.com/international/archive/2014/07/just-how-likely-is-another-world-war/375320/* with Robert Taber, *The War of the Flea,* Washington, DC: Brassey's Inc., 2002; George and Meredith Friedman, *The Future of War,* New York: Crown Publishers, 1996; John Mueller, *Retreat from Doomsday: The Obsolescence of Major War,* New York: Basic Books, 1989, available from *http://politicalscience.osu.edu/faculty/jmueller//doom.pdf*; and Evan Lard, *War in International Society,* New Haven: Yale University Press, 1987.

88. See Sharon Weinberg, "How To: Visit A Secret Nuclear Bunker," *Wired,* June 11, 2008, available from *http://www.wired.com/dangerroom/2008/06/how-to-visit-a/*; 20th Century Castles LLC, which sells decommissioned U.S. missile bases including bases for Atlas, Titan, and Nike missiles, available from *http://www.missilebases.com/properties*; GCI Datacentres, which uses NATO bunkers to secure and host computer servers, available from *http://gcichannelsolutions.com/products/data-centres/support-services.html*; and Siegfried Wittenburg, "A Warm Grave in a Cold War: East German Nuclear Bunker Opens to Tourists," *Spiegel Online International,* August 26, 2011, available from *http://www.spiegel.de/international/germany/a-warm-grave-in-a-cold-war-east-german-nuclear-bunker-opens-to-tourists-a-782755.html*. Burlington Bunker in Corsham, Wiltshire, UK, was formally a Cold War NATO nuclear bunker and is now a tourist sight, available from *http://www.burlingtonbunker.co.uk/* and guided tours of a missile launch facility and silo are offered by the National Park Service at the Minuteman Missile National Historic Site in South Dakota, available from *www.nps.gov/mimi/index.htm*.

The problem is that at least two states have not. U.S. intelligence agencies have determined that Russia invested over $6 billion to expand a 400 square mile underground nuclear complex at Yamantau a full decade *after* the Berlin Wall fell. This complex is burrowed deep enough to withstand a nuclear attack, and is large enough and provisioned sufficiently to house 60,000 people for months. U.S. intelligence officials believe it is one of a system of as many as 200 Russian nuclear bunkers (See Figure 8 below):[89]

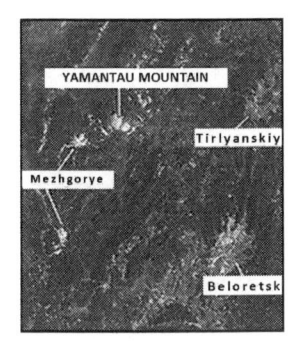

**Figure 8. Russian Underground Nuclear Complex at Yamantau.**[90]

China's nuclear passive-defense is no less impressive. In 2009, China's strategic missile command, the 2nd Artillery Corp, revealed that it had completed 3,000 miles of dispersed, deep, underground tunnels for the deployment of its nuclear-capable cruise and ballistic missile forces. China spent enormous sums to build this system and is still expanding the complex,

---

89. See "Yamantau," *GlobalSecurity.org*, available from *http://www.globalsecurity.org/wmd/world/russia/yamantau.htm*; "What's Going on in the Yamantau Mountain Complex?" *Viewzone*, available from *http://www.viewzone.com/yamantau.html*; Bill Gertz, "Russia Building New Underground Nuclear Command Posts," *Washington Free Beacon*, August 15, 2016, available from *http://freebeacon.com/national-security/russia-building-new-underground-nuclear-command-posts/*; and note 54.

90. Ibid.

which is known as the Underground Great Wall. The system is said to be designed and provisioned to house thousands of military staff during a nuclear exchange (see Figure 9 below):[91]

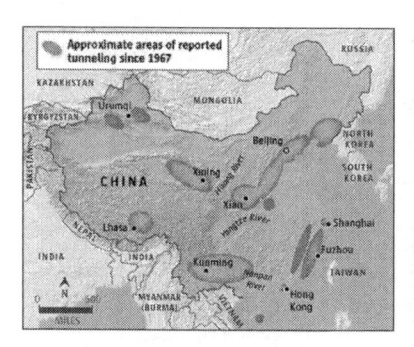

**Figure 9. China's Underground Great Wall.**[92]

North Korea also has gone to extensive lengths to protect its strategic assets. Almost all of its nuclear and long-range military systems have underground tunneled bases or host areas. South Korean intelligence estimates that North Korea has an excess of 10,000 underground facilities to protect its key military and civilian assets.[93]

---

91. See James R. Holmes, "China's Underground Great Wall," *The Diplomat*, August 20, 2011, available from *http://www.the-diplomat.com/flashpoints-blog/2011/08/20/chinas-underground-great-wall/*; Bret Stephens, "How Many Nukes Does China Have?" *Wall Street Journal*, October 24, 2011, available from *http://online.wsj.com/article/SB10001424052970204346104576639502894496030.html*; and William Wan, "Georgetown Students Shed Light on China's Tunnel System for Nuclear Weapons," *Washington Post*, November 29, 2011, available from *http://www.washingtonpost.com/world/national-security/georgetown-students-shed-light-on-chinas-tunnel-system-for-nuclear-weapons/2011/11/16/gIQA6AmKAO_story.html*.

92. See Wan, "Georgetown Students Shed Light on China's Tunnel System for Nuclear Weapons."

93. See Barbara Demick, "Thousands of North Korean Tunnels Hide Arms Secrets," *Los Angeles Times*, November 15, 2003, available from *http://community.seattletimes.nwsource.com/archive/?date=20031115&slug=koreacaves140*.

## *Going Ballistic*

All of this suggests that several nuclear-armed states still believe they may have to endure or engage in nuclear exchanges. Fortifying this suspicion is the increasing capacity states have to deliver both nuclear and nonnuclear payloads quickly against one another. Back in 1962, only the United States and Russia had nuclear-capable missile systems—i.e., cruise or ballistic missile systems capable of delivering a first-generation nuclear warhead (which would weigh 500 kilograms) 300 kilometers or farther.[94] Now, no fewer than 24 countries have perfected or acquired such systems, and nine can launch a satellite into orbit—i.e., have mastered all that's needed to deploy an intercontinental ballistic missile (ICBM). In addition, the United States, China, Iran, South Korea, Israel, and key NATO states are all working on precision conventional missiles capable of knocking out large military bases and major naval surface combatants that only a few decades ago were difficult or impossible to destroy *without* using nuclear weapons.[95] More nuclear-capable missile states are likely to emerge (see Figure 10 on the next page):

---

94. This definition of nuclear-capable missiles here is drawn directly from the Missile Technology Control Regime (MTCR). See *Missile Technology Control Regime (MTCR) Annex Handbook* (2010), pp. 1-3, available from *http://www.mtcr.info/english/MTCR_Annex_Handbook_ENG.pdf*.

95. See, e.g., Ian Easton and Mark Stokes, "China and the Emerging Strategic Competition in Aerospace Power," in *The Next Arms Race*, pp. 141-175, available from *http://npolicy.org/books/Next_Arms_Race/Ch5_Stokes-Easton.pdf* and Thomas Shugart, "Has China Been Practicing Preemptive Missile Strikes Against U.S. Bases?" *War on the Rocks*, February 6, 2017, available from *https://warontherocks.com/2017/02/has-china-been-practicing-preemptive-missile-strikes-against-u-s-bases/#*.

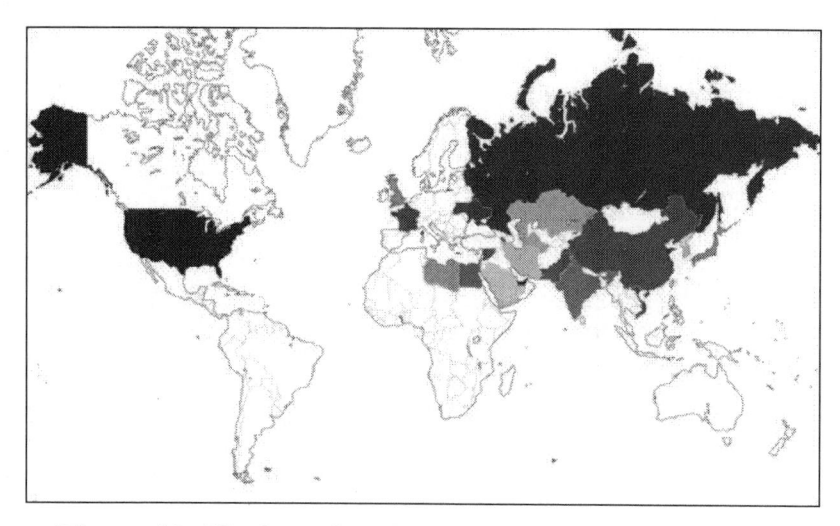

**Figure 10. Nuclear-Capable Missile Countries Today.**[96]

The strategic uncertainties these missile trends can generate are difficult to exaggerate. First, the proliferation of long-range missiles allows many more countries to play in any given regional dispute. One way to measure a state's diplomatic potential to influence others militarily is simply to map out the range arcs of its deployed missiles. Today, increasingly, these arcs and the diplomatic-political "power" shadows they cast overlap. Consider Iran. Its missiles now target Israel, Egypt, the UAE, Russia, Pakistan, France, Saudi Arabia, China, and the UK.

This is a very different world than that of a half-century ago. In 1962, when alliance loyalties within the Communist and Free World Blocs were at their height, only Russia and America had missiles aimed at each other. Now, there is no Communist Bloc, what remains of the Free World alliance system (e.g., NATO; Australia, New Zealand, United States Security Treaty [ANZUS], etc.) is relatively weak, and nuclear-capable missiles in hotspots like the Persian Gulf could be fired from any number of states—both near and far. For nuclear-

---

96. See note 81.

armed states, this situation places a premium on protecting their nuclear weapons-related systems against surprise attack.[97] It also raises first-order questions about nuclear escalation, which brings us to the second reason more missiles in more hands is a major worry: These missiles also can act as conventional catalysts for nuclear wars.

Increasingly, with precision guidance and advanced munitions technologies, it is possible to destroy targets that once required nuclear weapons—e.g., large air strips and air fields, command centers, naval ports, and even large, moving surface ships—with a handful of precise, conventionally-armed missiles instead. This has raised the prospect of states being able to knock out a significant portion of an opponent's key military forces *without* having to use nuclear weapons.[98]

The good news is that this should make the initial use of nuclear weapons less likely. The bad news is that with enough precision guidance capabilities, a state might be tempted to initiate combat in the expectation of winning without ever having to go nuclear and end up miscalculating badly.

---

97. On the vulnerability of U.S. strategic command and control systems and its land base ballistic missile force, see, e.g., Bill Gertz, "Stratcom: China Continuing to Weaponize Space with Latest Anti-Satellite Missile Shot," *Washington Free Beacon*, August 13, 2014, available from http://freebeacon.com/national-security/stratcom-china-continuing-to-weaponize-space-with-latest-anti-satellite-missile-shot/ and Bruce Sugden, "China's Conventional Strikes against the U.S. Homeland," *Center for International Maritime Security*, accessed August 18, 2014, available from http://cimsec.org/china-conventional-strike-us/11829.

98. There are, of course, limits to how far one can substitute conventional for nuclear munitions. See Steven Lukasik, "To What Extent Can Precision Conventional Technologies Substitute for Nuclear Weapons?" in *The Next Arms Race*, 387-412, available from http://npolicy.org/books/Next_Arms_Race/Ch12_Lukasik.pdf.

## War Scenarios

A real-world case, much discussed by Pakistani security analysts, is the mid-term prospect of an Indian conventional missile decapitation of Pakistani nuclear strategic command and control centers. The Indians, in this scenario, would use precise, offensive, long-range missiles to knock these centers out. Then, New Delhi could deter any remaining Pakistani retaliatory nuclear strike with India's much larger nuclear forces and with Indian nonnuclear missile defenses. Finally, India could prevail against Pakistani armor and artillery, with superior Indian military conventional forces.

To hedge against this prospect, Pakistan has ramped up its nuclear arms production and is deploying its nuclear weapons in ways designed to complicate Indian efforts to knock them out (e.g., delegation of launch authority under certain circumstances, forward deployment, dispersal, mobility, etc.). All of these methods only increase the prospects for nuclear use and have goaded India to develop new nuclear options of its own.

Beyond this, advanced conventional weapons might ignite a nuclear conflict directly. Again, consider India and Pakistan. After being hit by so many Pakistani-backed terrorist attacks, the Indian government has developed a conventional counterstrategy known as "Cold Start." Under this approach, India would respond to Pakistan-backed terrorist attacks by quickly seizing a limited amount of Pakistani territory, with quick alert, forward deployed Indian forces (i.e., that could launch from what Indian military planners call a cold start). The idea here would be to threaten to take a limited amount of territory that Pakistan holds dear, but not enough to prompt Pakistan to attack India with its nuclear weapons.

Unfortunately, India's adoption of a Cold Start plan has had nearly the reverse effect. Shortly after New Delhi broached this strategy,

Pakistani military officials announced their intent to use tactical nuclear weapons against any invading Indian force and deployed new, short-range nuclear-capable tactical missiles along the Pakistani-Indian border precisely for this purpose. India has responded by deploying tactical missiles of its own. It is unclear just how serious either India or Pakistan are about carrying out these war plans but this uncertainty is itself a worry.[99]

Of course, relying on nuclear weapons to counter conventional threats is not unique to Pakistan. Moscow, faced with advanced

---

99. See Zachary Keck, "India, 'Cold Start' and Pakistani Tactical Nukes," *The Diplomat*, May 8, 2013, available from *http://thediplomat.com/2013/05/india-cold-start-and-pakistani-tactical-nukes/*; Ajai Shukla, "Army's 'Cold Start' Doctrine Gets Teeth," *Business Standard*, July 22, 2011, available from *http://www.business-standard.com/article/economy-policy/army-s-cold-start-doctrine-gets-teeth-111072200071_1.html*; Muhammad Aslam Khan Niazi, "India Toying with Dangerous Cold Start War Doctrine," *Eurasia Review*, October 29, 2011, available from *http://www.eurasiareview.com/29102011-india-toying-with-dangerous-cold-start-war-doctrine-analysis/*; Ali Ahmed, "India and Pakistan: Azm-e-Nau as a Response to the Cold Start," *Institute of Pace and Conflict Studies*, July 28, 2013, available from *http://www.ipcs.org/article/india/india-and-pakistan-azm-e-nau-as-a-response-to-4056.html*; Muhammad Azam Khan, "India's Cold Start Is Too Hot;" Mike Mazza, "Pakistan's Strategic Myopia: Its Decision to Field Tactical Nuclear Weapons Will Only Make the Subcontinent More Unstable," *Wall Street Journal*, April 2011, available from *http://online.wsj.com/article/SB10001424052748704099704576288763180683774.html?mod=googlenews_wsj*; "Pakistan Army to Preempt India's 'Cold Start Doctrine,'" *Express Tribune*, June 16, 2013, available from *http://tribune.com.pk/story/564136/pakistan-army-to-preempt-indias-cold-start-doctrine/*; Dinakar Peri, "Nirbhay Will Be Backbone of 'Cold Start,' Say Experts," *The Hindu*, October 24, 2014, available from *http://www.thehindu.com/news/national/nirbhay-will-be-backbone-of-coldstart-say-experts/article6529087.ece*; Zahid Giskori, "LoC Skirmishes: Lawmaker Raises the Spectre of Nuclear War," *The Express Tribune*, October 23, 2014, available from *http://tribune.com.pk/story/779830/loc-skirmishes-lawmaker-raises-the-spectre-of-nuclear-war/*; and Henry Sokolski, "Civil Nuclear Cooperation with Pakistan: Prospects and Consequences," testimony given December 8, 2015, before the House Committee on Foreign Affairs' Subcommittee on Terrorism, Nonproliferation, and Trade, available from *http://www.npolicy.org/article.php?aid=1301&rtid=8*.

Chinese and NATO conventional forces, has also chosen to increase its reliance on tactical nuclear weapons. For Russia, employing these weapons is far less stressful economically than trying to field advanced conventional forces and is militarily pragmatic, given Russia's shrinking cohort of eligible military servicemen. China, in response, may be toying with deploying additional tactical nuclear systems of its own.[100]

## China and the Nuclear Rivalries Ahead

All of these trends are challenging. They also suggest what the next strategic arms competition might look like. First, if the United States and Russia maintain or reduce their current level of nuclear weapons deployments, it is possible that at least one other nuclear weapons state may be tempted to close the gap. Of course, in the short and even mid-term, Pakistan, Israel, and India could not hope to catch up. For these states, getting ahead of the two superpowers would

---

100. See, e.g., Jacob W. Kipp, "Asian Drivers of Russian Nuclear Force Posture," in *The Next Arms Race*, pp. 45-82, available from *http://npolicy.org/books/Next_Arms_Race/Ch2_Kipp.pdf*; Mark B. Schneider, "The Nuclear Forces and Doctrine of the Russian Federation and the People's Republic of China," testimony given October 12, 2011, before the House Armed Services Subcommittee on Strategic Forces, available from *http://www.worldaffairscouncils.org/2011/images/insert/Majority%20Statement%20and%20Testimony.pdf*; Nikolai N. Sokov, "Why Russia Calls a Limited Nuclear Strike 'De-escalation,'" *Bulletin of the Atomic Scientists*, March 13, 2014, available from *http://thebulletin.org/why-russia-calls-limited-nuclear-strike-de-escalation*; Graham Ong-Webb, "Power Posturing: China's Tactical Nuclear Stance Comes of Age," *Jane's Intelligence Review*, September 2010, pp. 47-55, available from *http://www.academia.edu/412039/Power_Posturing_Chinas_Tactical_Nuclear_Stance_Comes_of_Age_September_2010_*; Nicolas Giacometti, "Could China's Nuclear Strategy Evolve?" *The Diplomat*, October 16, 2014, available from *http://thediplomat.com/2014/10/could-chinas-nuclear-strategy-evolve/*; and Jonathan Ray, *Red China's "Capitalist Bomb": Inside the Chinese Neutron Bomb Program*, China Strategic Perspectives, no. 8, Washington, DC: National Defense University Press, 2015, available from *inss.ndu.edu/Portals/68/Documents/stratperspective/china/ChinaPerspectives-8.pdf*.

take great effort and at least one to three decades of continuous, flat-out military nuclear production. It is quite clear, moreover, that none of these states have set out to meet or beat the United States or Russia as a national goal.

China, however, is a different matter. It clearly sees the United States as a key military competitor in the Western Pacific and in Northeast Asia. China also has had border disputes with India and historically has been at odds with Russia as well. It is not surprising, then, that China has actively been modernizing its nuclear-capable missiles to target key U.S. and Indian military air and sea bases with advanced conventional missiles, and is developing even more advanced missiles to threaten U.S. carrier task forces on the open seas. In support of such operations, China is also modernizing its military space assets, which include military communications, command, surveillance, and imagery satellites and an emerging antisatellite capability.[101]

Then there is China's nuclear arsenal. For nearly 30 years, most respected Western security analysts have estimated the number of deployed Chinese nuclear warheads to be between 190 and 300.[102]

---

101. Brian Chow, "Avoiding Space War Needs a New Approach," *Defense News*, September 16, 2015, available from *http://www.defensenews.com/story/defense/commentary/2015/09/16/avoiding-space-war-needs-new-approach/32523905/*; Ian Easton, *China's Evolving Reconnaissance-Strike Capabilities,* Arlington, VA: Project 2049, February 2014, available from *http://www.project2049.net/documents/Chinas_Evolving_Reconnaissance_Strike_Capabilities_Easton.pdf*; Mark A. Stokes and Ian Easton, *Evolving Aerospace Trends in the Asia-Pacific Region,* Arlington, VA: Project 2049, May 27, 2010, available from *https://project2049.net/documents/aerospace_trends_asia_pacific_region_stokes_easton.pdf*; and Elbridge Colby, "Welcome to China and America's Nuclear Nightmare," *The National Interest,* December 19, 2014, available from *http://nationalinterest.org/feature/welcome-china-americas-nuclear-nightmare-11891.*

102. Cf. Kristensen and Norris, "Chinese Nuclear Forces, 2013" and Gertz, "The Warhead Gap."

Yet, by any account, China has produced enough weapons-usable plutonium and uranium to make up to four times this number of weapons. Why, then, have Chinese nuclear deployments been judged to be so low?

First, China has experienced first-hand what might happen if its nuclear weapons fell into the wrong hands. During the Cultural Revolution, one of its nuclear weapons laboratories test fired a nuclear-armed medium-range missile over heavily populated regions of China and exploded the device. Not long after, Mao ordered a major consolidation of China's nuclear warheads and had them placed under much tighter centralized control. Arguably, the fewer nuclear warheads China has, the easier it is for its officials to maintain control over them.[103]

Second, and possibly related, is China's declared nuclear weapons strategy. In its official military white papers since 2006 and in other forums, Chinese officials insist that Beijing would never be first to use nuclear weapons and would never use them against any non-nuclear weapons state. China also supports a doctrine that calls for a nuclear retaliatory response that is no more than what is "minimally" required for its defense. Most Western Chinese security experts have interpreted these statements to mean Beijing is interested in holding only a handful of opponents' cities at risk. This, in turn, has encouraged Western officials to settle uncertainties regarding Chinese nuclear warhead numbers toward the low end.[104]

---

103. See Mark Stokes, "Securing Nuclear Arsenals: A Chinese Case Study," in Henry Sokolski, ed., *Nuclear Weapons Security Crises: What Does History Teach?* Carlisle, PA: Strategic Studies Institute, 2013, pp. 65-85, available from http://npolicy.org/books/Security_Crises/Ch3_Stokes.pdf.

104. On China's no first use policies, see China's 2008 White Paper, "China's National Defense in 2008," available from http://www.fas.org/programs/ssp/nukes/2008DefenseWhitePaper_Jan2009.pdf; also see analysis of this paper by Hans M. Kristensen, "China Defense White Paper Describes Nuclear Escalation," *FAS Strategic Security Blog*, January 23, 2009, available from http://fas.org/

What China's actual nuclear use policies might be, though, is open to debate. As one analyst quipped, with America's first use of nuclear weapons against Japan in 1945, it is literally impossible for any country other than the United States to be first in using these weapons. More important, Chinese officials have emphasized that Taiwan is not an independent state and that under certain circumstances, it may be necessary for China to use nuclear weapons against this island "province." Also, there are the not-so-veiled nuclear threats that senior Chinese generals have made against the United States if it should use conventional weapons against China in response to a Chinese attack against Taiwan (including the observation that the United States would not be willing to risk Los Angeles to save Taipei).[105]

Finally, as China deploys more land-mobile and submarine-based nuclear missile systems, there will be increased technical and bureaucratic pressures to delegate more launch authority to each of China's military services. China's ballistic missile submarines already have complete nuclear systems under the command of their respective submarine captains. As China deploys ever more advanced road-mobile nuclear missiles, their commanders may want to have similar authority. Historically, in the United States

---

*blogs/security/2009/01/chinapaper/*; and M. Taylor Ravel and Evan S. Medeiros, "China's Search for Assured Retaliation: The Evolution of Chinese Nuclear Strategy and Force Structure," *International Security* 32, no. 2, Fall 2010, pp. 48-87, available from *http://belfercenter.ksg.harvard.edu/files/Chinas_Search_for_Assured_Retaliation.pdf*.

105. See Danny Gittings, "General Zhu Goes Ballistic," *Wall Street Journal*, July 18, 2005, available from *http://online.wsj.com/news/articles/SB112165176626988025* and Mark Schneider, "The Nuclear Doctrine and Forces of the People's Republic of China," *Comparative Strategy* 28, no. 3, Spring 2009, pp. 244-270. Also see an earlier version, dated 2007, available from *http://www.nipp.org/wp-content/uploads/2014/12/China-nuclear-final-pub.pdf*.

and Russia, such delegation of launch authority came with increased nuclear weapons requirements.[106]

The second cause for conservatism in assessing China's arsenal is the extent to which estimates of the number of Chinese warheads have been tied to the observed number of Chinese nuclear weapons missile launchers. So far, the number of these launchers that have been seen has been relatively low. Moreover, few, if any, missile reloads are assumed for each of these missile launchers, and it is presumed that only a handful of China's missiles have multiple warheads. The number of battlefield nuclear weapons, such as nuclear artillery, are also presumed to be low or nonexistent.

All of this may be right, but there are reasons to wonder. The Chinese, after all, claim that they have built 3,000 miles of tunnels to hide China's nuclear-capable missile forces and related warheads and that China continues to build such tunnels. Employing missile reloads for mobile missile systems has been standard practice for Russia and the United States. It would be odd if it was not also a Chinese practice, particularly given China's growing number of land-mobile solid-fueled rocket and cruise missile systems. With China's recent development of the DF-41, a massive, mobile, nuclear-armed ICBM, and its deployment of multiple independently targetable re-entry vehicles (MIRVs) on its silo-based DF-5s, U.S. authorities believe China is deploying a new generation of MIRVed missiles.[107] Also, as already noted, several experts believe China

---

106. See note 143 and Mark Stokes, "China's Future Nuclear Force Infrastructure: A Notional Breakout Scenario," draft paper prepared for the Nonproliferation Policy Education Center East Asian Alternative Nuclear Weapons Futures Conference, Honolulu, Hawaii, February 21, 2014, available from *http://npolicy.org/article_file/Stokes_-_CHINA_NUCLEAR_EXPANSION_SCENARIO.pdf*.

107. See Office of the Secretary of Defense, *Annual Report to Congress: Military and Security Developments Involving the People's Republic of China 2015*, Washington, DC: U.S. Department of Defense, 2015, available from *http://www.defense.gov/pubs/2015_China_Military_Power_Report.pdf*; David E. Sanger and

may be considering battlefield artillery for the delivery of tactical nuclear shells.

Precisely how large is China's nuclear arsenal, then? The answer is unclear. The Chinese say they are increasing the size of their nuclear weapons arsenal "appropriately."[108] They have not yet said by how much. General Viktor Yesin, the former chief of Russia's strategic rocket forces, in 2012 told U.S. security experts that China may have more than 900 deployed nuclear weapons and another 900 nuclear weapons stored in reserve.[109] This estimate, which is roughly seven times greater than most analysts believe Beijing possesses, would give China roughly as many warheads as the United States currently has deployed.[110]

---

William J. Broad, "China Making Some Missiles More Powerful," *The New York Times*, May 16, 2015, available from *http://www.nytimes.com/2015/05/17/world/asia/china-making-some-missiles-more-powerful.html?_r=0*; Tong Zhao and David Logan, "What if China Develops MIRVs?" *Bulletin of the Atomic Scientists*, March 24, 2015, available from *http://thebulletin.org/what-if-china-develops-mirvs8133*; and Bill Gertz, "China Adds Warheads to Older DF-5s," *The Washington Times*, February 10, 2016, available from *http://www.washingtontimes.com/news/2016/feb/10/inside-the-ring-china-adds-warhead-to-older-df-5s/*.

108. See *South China Morning Post*, "China 'Increasing Number of Missile Warheads,'" August 4, 2014, available from *http://www.scmp.com/news/china/article/1566294/china-increasing-number-missile-warheads*.

109. See U.S.-China Economic and Security Review Commission, *2012 Report to Congress,* Washington, DC: GPO, November 2012, pp. 170-214, available from *http://origin.www.uscc.gov/sites/default/files/annual_reports/2012-Report-to-Congress.pdf*; Gertz, "The Warhead Gap;" and "Nuclear Weapons: China's Nuclear Forces," *GlobalSecurity.org*, July 7, 2014, available from *http://www.globalsecurity.org/wmd/world/china/nuke.htm*.

110. A sharp critic of recent estimates that China might have as many as 3,000 nuclear weapons, though, was hardly reassuring in emphasizing that China could only "theoretically" have as many as 1,660 nuclear weapons. For more on this controversy, see Hans Kristensen, "No, China Does Not Have 3,000 Nuclear Weapons," *FAS Strategic Security Blog*, December 3, 2011, available from

Putting aside how accurate this Russian projection might be, the first problem it and other larger estimates present is how sound long-term U.S. and Russian strategic plans might be. It hardly is in Washington's or Moscow's interest to let Beijing believe it could threaten Taiwanese, Japanese, American, Indian, or Russian targets conventionally because China's nuclear forces were so large Beijing could assume they would deter any of these states from ever responding militarily (see Figure 11 below):

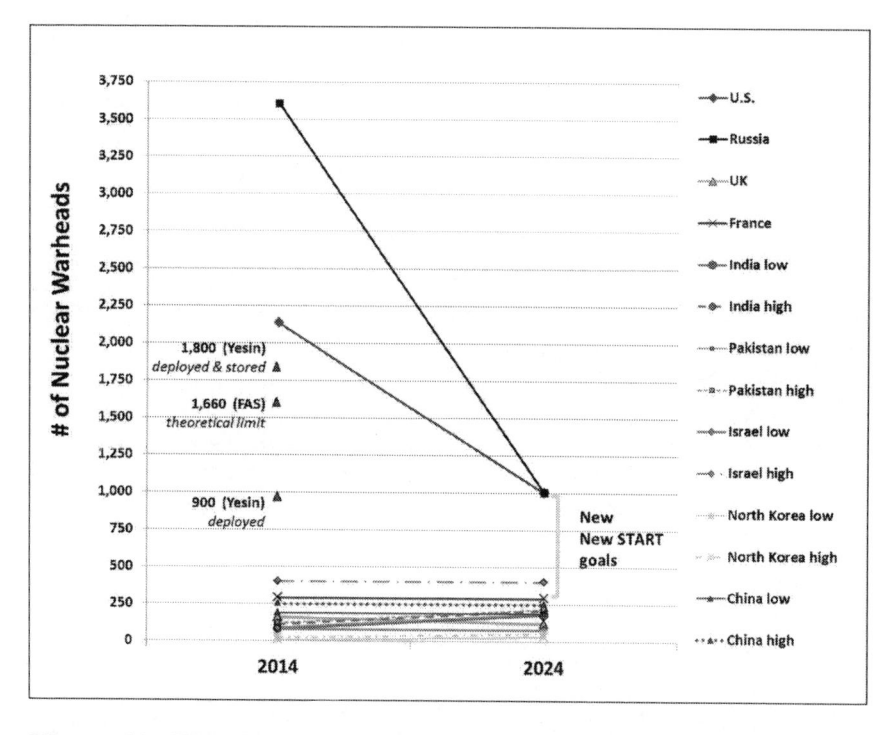

Figure 11. The Next Decade: Nuclear Weapons Uncertainties.[111]

---

http://fas.org/blogs/security/2011/12/chinanukes/.

111. The numbers used to generate this chart came from the sources listed in endnotes 70-72, plus Robert Burns, "US weighing steep nuclear arms cuts," *Associated Press,* February 14, 2012, available from *http://www.boston.com/ news/nation/washington/articles/2012/02/14/ap_newsbreak_us_weighing_ steep_nuclear_arms_cuts/*; and Kristensen, "No, China Does Not Have 3,000 Nuclear Weapons."

Yet another question that a much larger Chinese nuclear strategic force would raise is how it might impact future U.S.-Russian strategic arms negotiations. As China has increased its deployments of highly precise, nuclear-capable missile systems, Moscow has chaffed at the missile limits that the Intermediate-Range Nuclear Forces Treaty (INF Treaty) imposes on it fielding similar systems. Since the conclusion of New START in 2011, Moscow has balked at making any further cuts unless China is included in the negotiations. Shortly after several U.S. security analysts and members of Congress spotlighted Russian moves to break out of the INF Treaty,[112] the State Department announced that Russia had, in fact, violated the treaty.[113] American hawks, meanwhile, have warned against the United States making further nuclear cuts lest other states, like China, quickly ramp up their force levels to meet or exceed ours. Yet, President Trump has voiced a desire to do so.[114] All of this suggests the imperative for Washington and Moscow to factor China into their arms control and strategic modernization calculations. The question is how.

---

112. See Bill Gertz, "McKeon: State Department Ignores Major Russian Treaty Violation: Intermediate-range Nuclear Forces Treaty Breached," *Washington Free Beacon*, July 15, 2014, available from *http://freebeacon.com/national-security/mckeon-state-department-ignores-major-russian-treaty-violation/* and Jim Thomas, "Statement before the House Armed Services Subcommittee on Strategic Forces on the Future of the INF Treaty," July 17, 2014, available from *http://www.csbaonline.org/wp-content/uploads/2014/07/Thomas-INF-testimony1.pdf*.

113. See Michael R. Gordon, "U.S. Says Russia Tested Cruise Missile, Violating Treaty," *The New York Times,* July 28, 2014, available from *http://www.nytimes.com/2014/07/29/world/europe/us-says-russia-tested-cruise-missile-in-violation-of-treaty.html*.

114. See William James, "Trump says wants nuclear arsenals cut 'very substantially,'" *Reuters*, January 15, 2017, available from *http://www.reuters.com/article/us-usa-trump-russia-arms-idUSKBN14Z0XS* and Guy Faulconbridge and William James, "Trump's offer to Russia: an end to sanctions for nuclear arms cut - London Times," *Reuters*, January 16, 2017, available from *http://www.reuters.com/article/us-usa-trump-russia-arms-deal-idUSKBN14Z0YE*.

## Other Interested Parties

Unfortunately, getting a sound answer to this question is not possible without first considering the security concerns of states other than the United States, Russia, and China. Japan, for one, is an interested party. It already has roughly 2,000 weapons' worth of separated plutonium on its soil. This plutonium was supposed to fuel Japan's light water and fast reactors, a fleet which, before the accident at Fukushima, consisted of 54 reactors. After the accident, Japan shut down all of these plants, decided to reduce its reliance on nuclear power as much as possible, and is projected in the mid-term to bring no more than one-third of its light water reactor fleet back online.[115] Meanwhile, Japan's fast reactor program has been effectively frozen since the 1990s due to a series of accidents. Japan, the United States, and France plan on cooperating on a renewed effort but it is unlikely that a new fast reactor will be operating in Japan for decades.[116]

A related and immediate operational question is whether or not Japan will bring a $20-billion-plus commercial nuclear spent fuel reprocessing plant capable of producing roughly 1,500 bombs' worth of plutonium a year at Rokkasho online sometime in the fall of 2018. This plutonium recycling effort has been controversial. The original decision to proceed with it was made under Prime Minister Nakasone

---

115. See Mari Saito, Aaron Sheldrick and Kentaro Hamada, "Japan may only be able to restart one-third of its nuclear reactors," *Reuters,* April 2, 2014, available from *http://www.reuters.com/article/2014/04/02/us-japan-nuclear-restarts-insight-idUSBREA3020020140402*. In private interviews with several leading Japanese nuclear experts, the range of restarts given is somewhat higher—between 15-25 light water reactors. As of January 31, 2017, only two reactors were operating in Japan.

116. See "France and Japan Announce Cooperation on Generation IV Astrid FBR," *NucNet*, May 6, 2014, available from *http://www.nucnet.org/all-the-news/2014/05/06/france-and-japan-announce-cooperation-on-generation-iv-astrid-fbr*.

and can be tied to Japanese considerations of developing a plutonium nuclear weapons option. Although this plant is not necessary for the management of Japan's spent fuel, the forward costs of operating it could run as high as $100 billion. It is expected to produce eight tons of weapons-usable plutonium annually— enough to produce nearly as many first-generation nuclear weapons as is contained in America's entire deployed nuclear force (see Figure 12 below):[117]

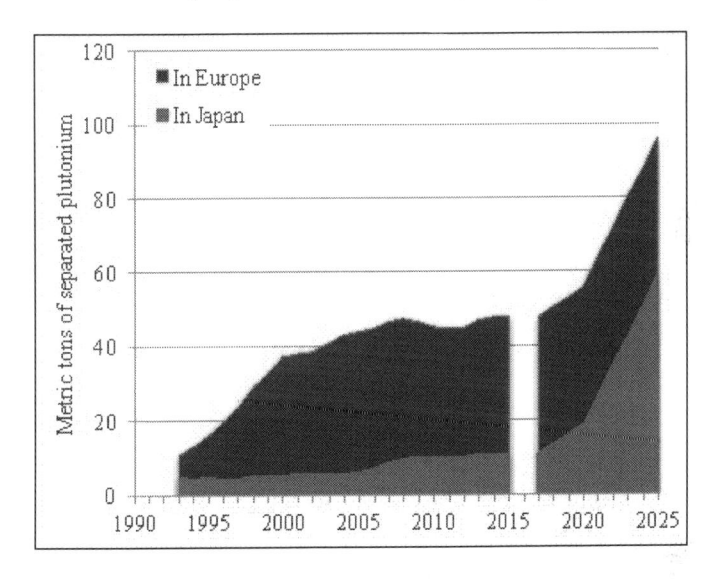

**Figure 12. Japanese Plutonium Stocks and Projected Production.**[118]

---

117. On these points, see von Hippel, "Plutonium, Proliferation and Radioactive-Waste Politics;" Henry Sokolski, "The Post-Fukushima Arms Race?" *Foreign Policy Online*, July 29, 2011, available from *http://www.foreignpolicy.com/articles/2011/07/29/the_post_fukushima_arms_race*; and Mari Yamaguchi, "Japan delays nuclear fuel reprocessing plant," *Associated Press*, November 16, 2015, available from *http://www.canadianmanufacturing.com/technology/japan-delays-nuclear-fuel-reprocessing-plant-157735/*.

118. See Frank von Hippel, Civilian Nuclear Fuel Cycles in Northeast Asia, paper presented the Panel on Peace and Security of North East Asia, Nagasaki, Japan, November 20, 2016, available from *http://npolicy.org/article_file/Civilian%20Nuclear%20Fuel%20Cycles%20in%20NE%20Asia%2028Oct2016%20*

In light of the questionable technical and economic benefits of operating Rokkasho, it would be difficult for Tokyo to justify proceeding with this plant's operation *unless* it wanted to develop an option to build a large nuclear weapons arsenal.[119] Given Japan currently retains nearly 11 tons of mostly reactor-grade plutonium on its soil, enough to make roughly 2,000 first-generation nuclear warheads, there is no immediate need to bring Rokkasho online to assure a military nuclear option.

However, Japan says it is committed to eliminating this surplus plutonium stockpile and recently surrendered roughly 800 kilograms of weapons-grade plutonium and uranium to the United States in pursuance of this stated goal.[120] In this context, keeping Rokkasho on the ready could be seen as a kind of national security insurance policy. Some leading Japanese figures clearly see it in this light[121]

---

%28rev.%202%29.pdf.

119. By the Japanese Atomic Energy Commission's own calculations made after the Fukushima accident, starting Rokkasho would only make sense over the next 20 to 30 years if more than 15 percent of Japan's electricity was produced by nuclear power reactors—i.e., 20 or more power reactors would have to be operating. As of the writing of this volume Japan had only two reactors online and it is unclear if the 15 percent criteria will ever be met. On this point, see note 109 and slides 24-30 from the presentation of former Japanese Atomic Energy Commission Vice Chairman, Tatsujiro Suzuki, "Nuclear Energy and Nuclear Fuel Cycle Policy Options, after the Fukushima Accident," presentation at the Nonproliferation Policy Education Center East Asian Alternative Energy Futures Conference, Honolulu, Hawaii, February 26, 2014, available from *http://npolicy.org/article_file/Suzuki-Japan-energy-nuclear-policy.pdf*.

120. See "Civilian HEU: Japan," Nuclear Threat Initiative, April 23, 2014, available from *http://www.nti.org/analysis/articles/civilian-heu-japan/* and "Japan to Send Weapons Grade Plutonium Back to U.S. this Weekend, Greenpeace Says," *Reuters*, March 18, 2016, available from *http://www.reuters.com/article/us-japan-nuclear-plutonium-idUSKCN0WK0VI*.

121. See note 75; Peter Symonds, "Is Japan Developing a Nuclear Weapons Program?" *Global Research*, May 7, 2013, available from *http://www.globalresearch.ca/is-japan-developing-a-nuclear-weapons-program/5334227*;

and technically, there is little question that the plutonium could be used to make effective weapons.[122] In this regard, even under a

---

Robert Windrem, "Japan Has Nuclear 'Bomb in the Basement,' and China Isn't Happy," *NBC News,* March 11, 2014, available from *http://www.nbcnews.com/storyline/fukushima-anniversary/japan-has-nuclear-bomb-basement-china-isnt-happy-n48976*; and Hiroko Tabuchi, "Japan Pushes Plan to Stockpile Plutonium, Despite Proliferation Risks," *The New York Times*, April 9, 2014, available from *http://www.nytimes.com/2014/04/10/world/asia/japan-pushes-plan-to-stockpile-plutonium-despite-proliferation-risks.html* where a former senior Japanese Trade Ministry official touts the deterrent value of having Rokkasho and separated plutonium on the ready. Also see, Elizabeth Shim, "Japan's Defense Chief Stands by Past Statement on Nuclear Armament," *UPI,* October 12, 2016, available from *http://www.upi.com/Top_News/World-News/2016/10/12/Japans-defense-chief-stands-by-past-statement-on-nuclear-armament/9541476297288/*.

122. Reactor-grade plutonium's tendency to spontaneously fission and to produce more heat than weapons-grade plutonium that has higher plutonium 239 and plutonium 241 isotopic content makes reactor-grade plutonium less than optimal for use in first-generation weapons designs of 1945. But as the U.S. Department of Energy noted in 1997, even assuming one used the crudest weapons design and fueled it with reactor-grade plutonium, yields "of the order of one or a few kilotons" could be expected. See note 73 and Robert Selden, "Reactor Plutonium and Nuclear Explosives," a slide presentation made before the Director General of the International Atomic Energy Agency in Vienna and before the Atomic Industrial Forum in Washington DC 1976, available from *http://nuclearpolicy101.org/wp-content/uploads/PDF/Selden_Reactor-Plutonium_slides.pdf*; Bruce Goodwin, "Reactor Plutonium Utility in Nuclear Explosives," brief given before a meeting at the New Diplomacy Initiative, Tokyo, Japan, November 6, 2015, available from *http://www.npolicy.org/article_file/Goodwin_Reactor-Plutonium-Utility.pdf*; U.S. Department of Energy, *Nonproliferation and Arms Control Assessment of Weapons-Usable Fissile Material Storage and Excess Plutonium Disposition Alternatives*, DOE/NN-0007, January 1997, pp. 37-39, available from *http://fissilematerials.org/library/doe97.pdf*; and J. Carson Mark, "Explosive Properties of Reactor-Grade Plutonium," *Science and Global Security* 4, no. 1, 1993, pp. 111-128, available from *http://scienceandglobalsecurity.org/archive/sgs04mark.pdf*. More important, weapons engineers today can readily compensate for these deficiencies. First, with highly precise missile delivery systems, the need for high-yield warheads to destroy point targets is dramatically reduced. As for destroying city centers, the difference between a 5 to 10 kiloton weapon and a 20 kiloton Nagasaki weapon is relatively small (this is because

much less nationalistic, pro-nuclear government than the one now in office, Japan's Diet in the fall of 2012 felt compelled to clarify in law that the purposes of the country's atomic energy program include supporting Japan's "national security."[123] Many nuclear

---

only a portion of the explosive power of any nuclear weapon exploded above a target impacts that target's surface plane) and even much smaller yield weapons would be quite destructive. Even at the very lowest range—at one-kiloton—the radius of destruction would still be roughly one-third that of the Hiroshima bomb. For a more detailed explanation of how increases in yield and aiming accuracies translate into increases in lethality, see Henry Sokolski and Kate Harrison, "Two Modern Military Revolutions: Dramatic Increases in Explosive Yields and Aiming Accuracies," Nonproliferation Policy Education Center, Arlington, VA, October 24, 2013, available from *http://nuclearpolicy101.org/wp-content/uploads/PDF/Two-Modern-Military-Revolutions.pdf*. Second, weapons designers can significantly mitigate most, if not all, of the heat and high neutron emission downsides of reactor-grade plutonium by utilizing warhead designs that the United States and Russia perfected and deployed over a half century ago—e.g., hollow cores, levitated pits, two-point ellipsoid designs, composite highly-enriched uranium-plutonium cores etc.—and using the latest high-explosive, heat management, and triggering technologies. These techniques would allow Japan to acquire relatively efficient, reliable yields using reactor-grade plutonium. Finally, more advanced designs that employ boosting with thermonuclear fuels, such as tritium, would entirely eliminate the neutron emission weapons design problems posed by reactor-grade plutonium. See Victor Gilinsky and Henry Sokolski, "The Other Dangers from That North Korean Nuke Test," *The Wall Street Journal*, January 19, 2016, available from *http://npolicy.org/article.php?aid=1304&rid=2*; David Albright and Serena Kelleher-Vergantini, "Update on North Korea's reactors, Enrichment Plant, and Possible Isotope Separation Facility," *Institute for Science and International Security*, February 1, 2016, available from *http://isis-online.org/isis-reports/detail/update-on-north-koreans-reactors-enrichment-plant-and-possible-isotope-sepa/*; Thomas B. Cochran, "Technological Issues Related to the Proliferation of Nuclear Weapons," presentation, Strategic Weapons Proliferation Teaching Seminar, San Diego, CA, August 23, 1998, available from *http://npolicy.org/article.php?aid=1310&tid=4*; and Gregory Jones, "Heavy Water Nuclear Power Reactors: A Source of Tritium for Potential South Korean Boosted Fission Weapons," Proliferation Matters, February 29, 2016, available from *http://nebula.wsimg.com/344f048726407b8951892db91c98a0b1?AccessKeyId=40C80D0B51471CD86975&disposition=0&alloworigin=1*.

123. See "Revisions to Japanese Atomic Law Cause Worry over Possible Weapons Aim," *Global Security Newswire*, June 22, 2012, available from *http://www.nti.*

observers outside of Japan saw this as a not-so-veiled reference to Japan's "civilian" plutonium-fuel cycle program.

Certainly, South Korean and Chinese officials and commentators spotlighted this prospect with concern.[124] Their apprehensions, then, raise the question: What might happen if Japan ever decided to open Rokkasho? How could this avoid stoking South Korean ambitions to make their own nuclear fuels? What of China's long-term efforts to modernize its own nuclear weapons systems and its "peaceful" scheme of building a copy of Rokkasho itself? Would not starting up Rokkasho only catalyze these efforts? What if Japan's startup of Rokkasho came after some Chinese or North Korean military provocation? Might this not trigger an additional round of Chinese, North Korean, and South Korean military and nuclear hedging actions?[125]

---

*org/gsn/article/revisions-japanese-atomic-law-spark-concern-about-possible-weapon-development/.*

124. See, e.g., "Alarm Over Nuke Stockpiles," *The Star Online*, October 25, 2015, available from *http://www.thestar.com.my/News/Regional/2015/10/25/Alarm-over-nuke-stockpiles-Japan-should-respond-to-concerns-of-the-international-community/*; Chinese Arms Control and Disarmament Association and the China Institute of Nuclear Information and Economics, "Study on Japan's Nuclear Material," September 2015, available from *http://www.cacda.org.cn/ueditor/php/upload/file/20151010/1444439848122903.pdf*; "S. Korea Could End Up Sandwiched Among Nuclear Powers," *Chosun Ilbo*, November 14, 2012, available from *http://english.chosun.com/site/data/html_dir/2012/06/29/2012062901173.html*; Austin Ramzy, "China Complains about Plutonium in Japan," *Sinosphere* (blog), *The New York Times*, June 10, 2014, available from *http://sinosphere.blogs.nytimes.com/2014/06/10/china-complains-about-plutonium-in-japan/?_php=true&_type=blogs&_r=0*; Liu Chong, "Japan's Plutonium Problem," *Beijing Review*, March 17, 2014, available from *http://www.bjreview.com.cn/world/txt/2014-03/17/content_607155.htm*; and Fredrick Dahl, "U.S. defends Japan against China's plutonium criticism," *Reuters*, March 5, 2014, available from *http://www.reuters.com/article/2014/03/05/us-japan-plutonium-usa-idUSBREA2421A20140305?irpc=932&irpc=932.*

125. See, e.g., Anna Fifield, "As North Korea Flexes its Muscles, Some in South Want Nukes, too," *The Washington Post*, March 20, 2016, available from

Yet another "peaceful" East Asian nuclear activity that bears watching is the substantial plans both Japan and China have to enrich uranium. Both countries justify these efforts as being necessary to fuel their light water reactor fleets. There are several difficulties with this argument, though. First, both countries already have access to foreign uranium enrichment services that are more than sufficient to supply current demand. Second, any effort to become commercially self-sufficient in enriching uranium in the name of "energy independence" is questionable for Japan and China given their lack of economic, domestic sources of high-grade uranium ore.

Even assuming China could stop importing enrichment services, as it now does from URENCO of Europe and Minatom/Tenex of Russia, then, it still would want to import much of its uranium ore from overseas. Of course, operating commercial enrichment capacity could afford bargaining leverage to secure cheaper foreign enrichment service contracts. But in China's case (and Japan's and South Korea's cases as well), such leverage can be had at enrichment capacities far below those they have or want to acquire. Again, both uranium ore and enrichment services are readily available globally at reasonable prices and are projected to remain so. Uranium yellowcake spot prices are currently at historic lows. As for enrichment services, the World Nuclear Association pegs the world's current surplus of uranium enrichment capacity to be well above international demand and projects supply will outstrip demand by nearly

---

*https://www.washingtonpost.com/world/asia_pacific/as-north-korea-flexes-its-muscles-the-other-korea-looks-at-nukes-too/2016/03/20/e2b1bb22-eb88-11e5-a9ce-681055c7a05f_story.html*; "S.Koreans Must Discuss Acquiring Nuclear Arms," *The Chosun Ilbo*, January 28, 2016, available from *http://english.chosun.com/site/data/html_dir/2016/01/28/2016012801950.html*; "'Seoul Temporarily Drop Out NPT,' says Chung Mong-joon," *The Dong-A Ilbo,* February 15, 2016, available from *http://english.donga.com/Home/3/all/26/525363/1*; and "U.S. would Back a Rethink of Japan's Plutonium Recycling Program: White House," *The Japan Times*, May 21, 2016, available from *http://www.japantimes.co.jp/news/2016/05/21/national/politics-diplomacy/u-s-back-rethink-japans-plutonium-recycling-program-white-house/#.V17f94SDGkr.*

50 percent through 2020.[126] In short, there is no lack of enrichment services internationally and, given China's access to Russian and European enrichers, there is little or no immediate economic imperative for building more.

China, however, sees things differently. It currently has enough capacity to fuel a dozen large reactors and is building more than enough centrifuges to fuel 58 gigawatts of nuclear capacity, optimistically projected to be online by 2020.[127] Some of this projected capacity may be set aside for possible reactor exports beyond those China is making to Pakistan. Yet, again, given the foreign enrichment services glut, none of this enrichment expansion makes much economic sense. What is all too clear, however, is just how much of a military option this enrichment capacity affords. By 2020, China's planned enrichment capacity could fuel all of its planned

---

126. On these points, see "Uranium Enrichment," World Nuclear Association, January 2015, available from *http://www.world-nuclear.org/info/Nuclear-Fuel-Cycle/Conversion-Enrichment-and-Fabrication/Uranium-Enrichment/*; Edward Kee and Jennifer Cascone Fauver, "ACP & World Enrichment Market," draft report, NERA Economic Consulting, Washington, DC, September 5, 2013, 25, available from *http://www.centrusenergy.com/sites/default/files/NERA_ACP_And_World_Enrichment_Market_0.pdf*; and Hui Zhang, "Uranium Supplies: A Hitch to China's Nuclear Energy Plans? Or Not?" *Bulletin of the Atomic Scientists*, May 4, 2015, available from *http://thebulletin.org/2015/may/uranium-supplies-hitch-chinas-nuclear-energy-plans-or-not8296*.

127. It should be noted that China may encounter difficulties in achieving its 2020 reactor capacity goal. See Mycle Schneider, Antony Froggatt, et al., *The World Nuclear Industry Status Report 2014*, Mycle Schneider Consulting, Paris, London, and Washington, DC, July 2014, 105-110, available from *http://www.worldnuclearreport.org/IMG/pdf/201408msc-worldnuclearreport2014-lr-v3.pdf*; David Stanway, "China Says First Westinghouse Reactor Delayed until At Least End-2015," *Reuters*, July 18, 2014, available from *http://www.reuters.com/article/2014/07/18/china-nuclear-ap-idUKL4N0PT0T820140718?irpc=932*; and Stephen Chen, "As China's Economy Matures, It Trades Speed for Build Quality on Big Projects," *South China Morning Post*, September 21, 2014, available from *http://www.scmp.com/news/china/article/1596995/chinas-economy-matures-it-trades-speed-build-quality-big-projects*.

civilian reactors and still produce additional material sufficient for more than 1,500 nuclear weapons a year.[128]

Japan's enrichment plans differ only in scale. Like China, it too lacks economic, domestic sources of high-grade uranium ore. As for Tokyo's current enrichment capacity, it can fuel about eight reactors a year. If Japan used all of this enrichment capacity for military purposes, it could make roughly 4,500 kilograms of weapons-grade uranium annually—enough to make at least 200 first-generation nuclear weapons.[129] Japan plans to upgrade its uranium enrichment centrifuges. The question, in light of the global surplus of commercial uranium enrichment capacity, though, is why (see Figure 13):

---

128. These estimates assume China would employ the advanced nuclear weapons designs it has clearly mastered and that, as such, only 12 kilograms of highly-enriched uranium would be needed per Chinese weapon. See note 80. On China's projected enrichment capability and plans, see Hui Zhang, Assessing China's Uranium Enrichment Capacity, Paper, Institute for Nuclear Materials Management 57th Annual Meeting, July 24-28, 2016, Atlanta, Georgia, USA, available from *http://belfercenter.ksg.harvard.edu/publication/26984/assessing_chinas_uranium_enrichment_capacity.html?breadcrumb=%2Fexperts%2F13%2Fhui_zhang* and World Nuclear Association, "Uranium Enrichment." For 2020, Zhang forecasts 13.5 million SWU per year.

129. This set of uranium weapons estimates conservatively assumes Japan would need 20 kilograms of highly-enriched uranium per weapon. It is possible, however, that Japan might need as little as 12 or 13 kilograms per weapon. See note 80. On Japan's enrichment capability, see WISE Uranium Project, "World Nuclear Fuel Facilities" and Frank Von Hippel, Civilian Nuclear Fuel Cycles in Northeast Asia, paper presented the Panel on Peace and Security of North East Asia, Nagasaki, Japan, November 20, 2016, available from *http://npolicy.org/article_file/Civilian%20Nuclear%20Fuel%20Cycles%20in%20NE%20Asia%2028Oct2016%20%28rev.%202%29.pdf*.

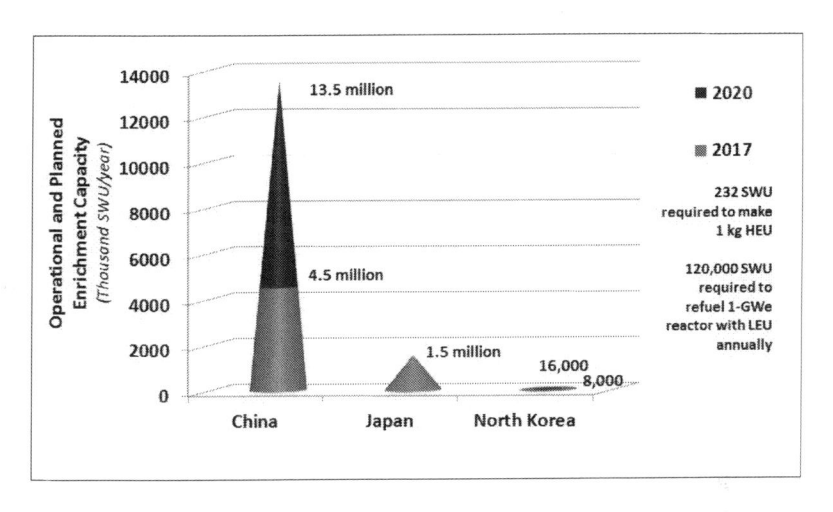

**Figure 13. Current and Projected East Asian Uranium Enrichment Capacities.**[130]

As noted, none of these Japanese nuclear fuel making activities and plans sit well with China or South Korea. Seoul, in a not so well-disguised security hedge, began to press Washington in 2009 for

---

130. For the number of SWU to make 1 kg HEU or refuel 1-GWe reactor, see Richard L. Garwin, "HEU Done It," Letter to the Editor of *Foreign Affairs*, March/April 2005, in response to an article by Selig S. Harrison, "'Did North Korea Cheat?" in *Foreign Affairs*, January/February 2005, available from *http://www.fas.org/rlg/030005HDI.pdf* and "Separative Work Unit (SWU)," World Nuclear Association Glossary, updated March 2014, available from *http://www.world-nuclear.org/Nuclear-Basics/Glossary/*. For China and Japan figures see notes 128 and 129. Reports from November 2014 indicate that North Korea began operating a new enrichment facility capable of doubling its existing 8,000 SWU/year enrichment capacity, but production of weapons-grade material at the new facility has not been confirmed. See David Albright and Robert Avagyan, "Recent Doubling of Floor Space at North Korean Gas Centrifuge Plant," *Institute for Science and International Security*, August 8, 2013, available from *http://isis-online.org/isis-reports/detail/recent-doubling-of-floor-space-at-north-korean-gas-centrifuge-plant/10*; and "North Korea puts new uranium enrichment facility into operation – media," *Tass*, November 5, 2014, available from *http://itar-tass.com/en/world/758055*.

permission to separate "peaceful" plutonium from U.S.-origin spent fuel and to enrich U.S.-origin uranium in Korea.

These requests coincided with several other South Korean security-related demands. The first came after North Korea's sinking of the *Cheonan* and the bombardment of Yeonpyeong Island. South Korean parliamentarians asked the United States to redeploy U.S. tactical nuclear weapons on Korean soil. Washington refused.[131] Then, Seoul pushed Washington to extend the range of its nuclear-capable missiles from 300 kilometers to 800 and practically be freed from range limits on its cruise missile and space satellite launchers. Washington relented.[132] As for South Korea's nuclear demands, Seoul is likely to continue to press its case.[133]

---

131. See Julian Borger, "South Korea Considers Return of U.S. Tactical Nuclear Weapons," *Guardian* (Manchester), November 22, 2010, available from http://www.guardian.co.uk/world/2010/nov/22/south-korea-us-tactical-weapons-nuclear; David Dombey and Christian Oliver, "US Rules Out Nuclear Redeployment in South Korea," *Financial Times*, March 1, 2011, available from http://www.ft.com/intl/cms/s/0/e8a2d456-43b0-11e0-b117-00144feabdc0.html#axzz4BZxYOR00; and Ser Myo-ja, "Bring Back U.S. Nukes, Says Blue House Report," *Korea Joongang Daily*, October 14, 2016, available from http://koreajoongangdaily.joins.com/news/article/Article.aspx?aid=3024895.

132. See Daniel Pinkston, "The New South Korean Missile Guidelines and Future Prospects for Regional Stability," *In Pursuit of Peace* (blog), International Crisis Group, October 25, 2012, available from http://blog.crisisgroup.org/asia/2012/10/25/the-new-south-korean-missile-guidelines-and-future-prospects-for-regional-stability/ and Jeffrey Lewis, "RoK Missile Rationale Roulette," *Arms Control Wonk* (blog), October 9, 2012, available from http://lewis.armscontrolwonk.com/archive/5771/rok-missile-rationale-roulette.

133. After more than five years of negotiations, the U.S. and South Korea finally agreed to a nuclear cooperative agreement in June 2015. This agreement initially prevents South Korea from reprocessing or enriching U.S.-origin nuclear materials. The agreement, however, also creates a consultative process that would allow South Korea to change this. There is good reason to believe that South Korea will continue to press its case for such a change. See James E. Platte, "Next Steps for U.S.-South Korea Civil Nuclear Cooperation," *Asia Pacific Bulletin*, July 1, 2015, available from http://www.eastwestcenter.org/system/tdf/private/

The question is what's next? Will Japan start Rokkasho as planned late in 2018? What commercial nuclear fuel making activities, if any, might Washington allow South Korea and China to engage in?[134] Will North Korea or China continue to engage in provocations that will increase Japanese or South Korean demands for more strategic military independence from their American security alliance partner?

The two popular rejoinders to these questions are that there is no reason to worry. Most experts insist that neither Japan nor South Korea would ever acquire nuclear weapons. The reasons, they argue, are simple. It would not only undermine the nuclear nonproliferation regime that they have sworn to uphold and strengthen, it would risk their continued security ties with their most important ally, the United States.

Perhaps, but when South Korea first doubted its American security guarantees in the 1970s, it tried to get nuclear weapons.[135] Those

---

*apb316_0.pdf?file=1&type=node&id=35218* and Soo Kim, *Proliferation Fallout from the Iran Deal: The South Korean Case Study,* Washington, DC: FDD Press, October 2015, available from *http://www.defenddemocracy.org/content/uploads/documents/Proliferation_Fallout_South_Korea.pdf*.

134. See Frank Von Hippel and Fumihiko Yoshida, "A Little-Known Nuclear Race Taking Place in East Asia Is Dangerous and Pointless," *Huffington Post*, April 5, 2016, available from *http://www.huffingtonpost.com/frank-von-hippel/nuclear-race-asia_b_9609116.html*; Henry Sokolski, "Can East Asia Avoid a Nuclear Explosive Materials Arms Race?" *Bulletin of the Atomic Scientists*, March 28, 2016, available from *http://thebulletin.org/can-east-asia-avoid-nuclear-explosive-materials-arms-race9295*; and Brad Sherman, Jeff Fortenberry, and Adam Schiff, "Letter to President Obama Regarding the Production of Fissile Material in East Asia," May 19, 2016, available from *http://npolicy.org/article.php?aid=1317&rtid=4*.

135. For a complete historiography of South Korea's nuclear weapons program, see Alexander Lanoszka, "Seoul in Isolation: Explaining South Korean Nuclear Behavior, 1968-1980," in *Protection States Trust?: Major Power Patronage, Nuclear Behavior, and Alliance Dynamics* (PhD. Dissertation,

doubts continue today as North Korea builds up its nuclear and nonnuclear forces against the South.[136] On May 29, 2014, South Korea's president noted that if North Korea tested another nuclear weapon, it would make it difficult "to prevent a nuclear domino from occurring in this area"—a clear warning not only to North Korea, but the United States and China, that if they fail to prevent Pyongyang from further perfecting its nuclear force, Japan and South Korea might well acquire nuclear weapons of their own.[137] After Pyongyang conducted its fourth nuclear test, on January 6, 2016, South Korean and Japanese politicians commented on the legality and desirability of developing nuclear weapons options.[138] They repeated these points when Pyongyang tested its fifth device later in 2016.[139]

Yet another optimistic view argues that it may actually be in Washington's interest to let Japan and South Korea go nuclear. Letting

---

Princeton University, 2010), available from *http://www.alexlanoszka.com/ AlexanderLanoszkaROK.pdf*.

136. See, e.g., Ted Galen Carpenter, "South Korea's Growing Nuclear Flirtation," *China-US Focus*, April 24, 2013, available from *http://www.chinausfocus.com/ peace-security/south-koreas-growing-nuclear-flirtation/*.

137. See Gerald Baker and Alastair Gale, "South Korea President Warns on Nuclear Domino Effect," *Wall Street Journal*, May 29, 2014, available from *http://online.wsj.com/articles/south-korea-president-park-geun-hye-warns-on-nuclear-domino-effect-1401377403*.

138. See Anna Fifield, "As North Korea Flexes its Muscles, Some in South Want Nukes, Too," *The Washington Post*, March 20, 2016, available from *https:// www.washingtonpost.com/world/asia_pacific/as-north-korea-flexes-its-muscles-the-other-korea-looks-at-nukes-too/2016/03/20/e2b1bb22-eb88-11e5-a9ce-681055c7a05f_story.html*.

139. For example after the fifth nuclear test, Rep. Won Yoo-chul from the ruling Saenuri Party said "We need to take steps to be armed with our own nuke not only to protect ourselves, but to preserve peace." See "Lawmakers call for nukes following N. Korea's 5th nuclear test," *Yonhap News*, September 9, 2016, available from *http://english.yonhapnews.co.kr/northkorea/2016/09/09/0401000000A EN20160909008151315.html*.

them arm might actually tighten America's relations with these key allies while reducing what the United States would otherwise have to spend for their protection. Implicit to this argument is the hope neither Seoul nor Tokyo would feel compelled to acquire many weapons—i.e., that like the UK, they would eagerly integrate their modest nuclear forces with that of America's larger force, share their target lists with Washington, and that Washington would do likewise with them (as Washington already has with London).[140]

Again, this is plausible. But it is worth noting that Japan and South Korea are not the UK. Early on, the UK understood its nuclear weapons efforts would ultimately be subordinate to and in the service of maintaining its "special relationship" with Washington (and scaled down its nuclear efforts accordingly). With the Japanese and South Koreans, though, their nuclear efforts would unavoidably be seen as a vote of no confidence in Washington's nuclear security guarantees. As such, these efforts would have to deal with demands by nationalists eager to build a truly independent nuclear force of much more ambitious dimensions.[141] More important (and

---

140. See note 24; Ian Easton, "Japanese Weapons Programs and Strategies: Future Scenarios and Alternative Approaches," Arlington, VA: The Nonproliferation Policy Education Center, 2015, available from *http://npolicy.org/books/East_Asia/Ch7_Easton.pdf*; and Charles D. Ferguson, "How South Korea Could Acquire and Deploy Nuclear Weapons," Arlington, VA: The Nonproliferation Policy Education Center, 2015, available from *http://npolicy.org/books/East_Asia/Ch4_Ferguson.pdf*.

141. When polled, roughly 10 percent of the Japanese electorate now identify themselves as New Rightists. Yet an additional percentage of Japanese may be sympathetic to the New Right. Japanese New Rightists now have their own organized political parties; the age of those who identify with these organizations is dropping; and, now, is much lower than it was a generation ago. More important, as Japan reforms its foreign and military policies, the political parties with the clearest views on these topics are the New Right. See, e.g., Yuka Hayashi, "Tension in Asia Stoke Rising Nationalism in Japan: Young Conservatives, Japan's Version of U.S. Tea Party, Are Fast Gaining Clout," *Wall Street Journal*, February 26, 2014, available from *http://online.wsj.com/articles/*

more likely), even if Japanese and South Korean officials wanted to keep their forces subordinate to those of the United States, they might still be driven to acquire larger nuclear forces of their own to deal with the likely military reactions of China, North Korea, and other nuclear states.[142]

Consider the action-reaction dynamic of Seoul or Tokyo going nuclear might set into motion with Beijing and Pyongyang. Presumably, in all cases (China included), each state would try to protect its strategic forces against possible attacks by building more passive defenses (hardening, mobility, tunneling, etc.). They also would focus on building up their offensive forces (both nuclear and non-nuclear) so they might eliminate as much of each other's strategic forces at sea and on land as soon as any war began (this to limit the damage they would otherwise suffer). Finally, they would increase the number of nuclear weapons assets, missile portals, and other strategic aim points to prevent any of their adversaries from thinking they could "knockout" their retaliatory forces. This, roughly, is what unfolded during the Cold War rivalry between Washington and the Soviet Union: As was the case for Russia and the United States then, maintaining one's relative nuclear position could easily drive up East Asian nuclear weapons requirements well beyond scores or even hundreds of weapons.[143]

---

*SB10001424052702304610404579403492918900378*; Kathryn Ibata-Arens, "Why Japan's Right Turn Could Be Trouble for the US," *Daily Beast,* December 16, 2012, available from *http://www.thedailybeast.com/articles/2012/12/16/why-japan-s-right-turn-could-be-trouble-for-the-u-s.html*; and Roland Kelts, "The Identity Crisis that Lurks Behind Japan's Right-Wing Rhetoric," *Time,* May 31, 2013, available from *http://world.time.com/2013/05/31/the-identity-crisis-that-lurks-behind-japans-right-wing-rhetoric/*.

142. See note 134.

143. At the height of the Cold War, the United States had over 31,000 nuclear weapons; the Soviets 40,000 (see note 26). Some senior military planners, however, considered even these high numbers to be insufficient. For example, in a recently declassified official Department of Defense history, it was revealed that

Potentially catalyzing this rivalry further are the actions China's immediate nuclear neighbors might take. As has already been noted, the Russians are unlikely to reduce their nuclear weapons deployments if the Chinese increase theirs. As for India, it already has roughly 100 nuclear weapons and many hundreds of bombs' worth of separated reactor-grade plutonium it claims it can fashion into nuclear weapons. It is hedging its nuclear bets even further with plans to build six unsafeguarded plutonium-producing breeder reactors by 2030 and an enrichment plant that may double its production of weapons-grade uranium.[144] Late in 2011, India announced it was working with Russia

---

the U.S. Army alone in 1956 had a requirement for 151,000 nuclear weapons. This suggests how nuclear warhead requirements might trend upward in an unconstrained East Asian nuclear weapons competition. See Office of the Assistant to the Secretary of Defense (Atomic Energy), *History of the Custody and Deployment of Nuclear Weapons: July 1945 through September 1977*, Washington, DC: U.S. Department of Defense, February 1978, p. 50, available from *http://www.dod.gov/pubs/foi/Reading_Room/NCB/306.pdf*. For a more detailed discussion of the demanding requirements for any state contemplating tactical weapons deployments today of the sort South Korea or China might choose to pursue, see Jeffrey D. McCausland, "Pakistan's Nuclear Weapons: Operational Myths and Realities," *Stimson Center Analysis*, March 10, 2015, available from *http://www.stimson.org/summaries/pakistans-tactical-nuclear-weapons-operational-myths-and-realities/*.

144. See Adrian Levy, "India is Building a Top-Secret Nuclear City to Produce Thermonuclear Weapons, Experts Say," *Foreign Policy*, December 16, 2015, available from *http://foreignpolicy.com/2015/12/16/india_nuclear_city_top_secret_china_pakistan_barc/* and International Panel on Fissile Materials, *Plutonium Separation in Nuclear Power Programs*. Also see "India to Commission Breeder Reactor in 2013," *New Indian Express*, February 20, 2012, available from *www.newindianexpress.com/nation/article322002.ece*; Paul Brannan, "Further Construction Progress of Possible New Military Uranium Enrichment Facility in India," Institute for Science and International Security, October 5, 2011, available from *http://www.isis-online.org/isis-reports/detail/further-construction-progress-of-possible-new-military-uranium-enrichment-f/7*; Douglas Busvine, "India Nuke Enrichment Plant Expansion Operational in 2015 – IHS," *Reuters*, June 20, 2014, available from *http://www.reuters.com/article/2014/06/20/india-nuclear-idINKBN0EV0JR20140620*; and "India Plans to Construct Six More Fast

to develop a terminally guided ICBM in response to Chinese medium-range ballistic missile deployments near India's borders.[145]

New Delhi has also pushed the development of a nuclear submarine force, submarine-launched ballistic missiles (SLBM), missile defenses, long-range cruise missiles, and improved strategic command and control and intelligence systems. India is not yet competing with China weapon-for-weapon. But if China were to increase its nuclear weapons deployments significantly, Indian leaders might argue that they had no other choice but to increase their own nuclear holdings.

This then brings us back to Pakistan. It has done all it can to keep up with India militarily. Since Islamabad is already producing as much plutonium and highly-enriched uranium as it can, it would likely seek further technical assistance from China and financial help from its close ally, Saudi Arabia. Islamabad may do this to hedge against India, whether China or India build their nuclear arms up or not. There is also good reason to believe that Saudi Arabia may want to cooperate on nuclear weapons-related activities with Pakistan or China to help Saudi Arabia hedge against Iran's growing nuclear weapons capabilities. It is unclear if either China or Pakistan would actually transfer nuclear weapons directly to Saudi Arabia or choose instead to merely

---

Breeder Reactors," *The Economic Times*, December 1, 2015, available from *http://articles.economictimes.indiatimes.com/2015-12-01/news/68688445_1_fuel-loading-prototype-fast-breeder-reactor-pfbr*.

145. "Russia to Provide 'Seeker' Tech for Agni-V ICBM," *Asian Defence News*, October 26, 2011, available from *http://www.asian-defence.net/2011/10/russia-to-provide-seeker-tech-for.html*; B. K. Pandey, "Agni-V to Be Launched By March End," SP's *Aviation.net*, available from *http://www.sps-aviation.com/story_issue.asp?Article=900*; and "Why Is This DRDO Official in Moscow?" *Trishul* (blog), October 5, 2011, available from *http://trishul-trident.blogspot.com/2011/10/why-is-this-drdo-official-in-moscow.html*.

help it develop aspects of a "peaceful" nuclear program, including reprocessing and enrichment. They might do both.[146]

In this regard, Saudi Arabia has made it known that it intends to build up its "peaceful" nuclear energy capabilities and will not forswear its "right" to enrich uranium or to reprocess plutonium. This would constitute one of the most lucrative, best financed near and mid-term nuclear power markets in the world. The reactors Saudi Arabia might build also could serve as the basis for development of a major nuclear weapons option. As Saudi Arabia's former head of intelligence told NATO ministers, the kingdom would have to get nuclear weapons if Iran did.[147]

---

146. See, e.g., Jeff Stein, "Exclusive: CIA Helped Saudis in Secret Chinese Missile Deal," *Newsweek*, January 29, 2014, available from *http://www.newsweek.com/exclusive-cia-helped-saudis-secret-chinese-missile-deal-227283*; Bill Gertz, "Saudi Arabia Shows Off Chinese Missiles," *Washington Free Beacon*, May 2, 2014, available from *http://freebeacon.com/national-security/saudi-arabia-shows-off-chinese-missiles/*; Mark Urban, "Saudi nuclear weapons 'on order' from Pakistan," *BBC News*, November 6, 2013, available from *http://www.bbc.com/news/world-middle-east-24823846*; "Report: Saudi Arabia to Buy Nukes if Iran Tests A-bomb," *MSNBC*, February 10, 2012, available from *http://worldnews.nbcnews.com/_news/2012/02/10/10369793-report-saudi-arabia-to-buy-nukes-if-iran-tests-a-bomb*; Andrew Dean and Nicholas A. Heras, "Iranian Crisis Spurs Saudi Reconsideration of Nuclear Weapons," *Terrorism Monitor* 10, no. 4, February 23, 2012, pp. 4-6, available from *http://www.jamestown.org/programs/gta/single/?tx_ttnews%5Btt_news%5D=39048&tx_ttnews%5BbackPid%5D=26&cHash=9aecde0ac8f6849d8877289c07a49ad7*; Mustafa Alani, "How Iran Nuclear Standoff Looks to Saudis," *Bloomberg View*, February 15, 2012, available from *http://www.bloombergview.com/articles/2012-02-16/how-iran-nuclear-standoff-looks-from-saudi-arabia-mustafa-alani*; and Ali Ahmad, "The Saudi Proliferation Question," *Bulletin of the Atomic Scientists,* December 17, 2013, available from *http://thebulletin.org/saudi-proliferation-question.*

147. See Jason Burke, "Riyadh Will Build Nuclear Weapons if Iran Gets Them, Saudi Prince Warns," *Guardian* (Manchester), June 29, 2011, available from *http://www.theguardian.com/world/2011/jun/29/saudi-build-nuclear-weapons-iran* and Angelina Rascouet and Wael Mahdi, "Saudi Arabia to Select Nuclear Power-Plant Site 'Very Soon'," *Bloomberg*, October 20, 2016, available from *http://www.bloomberg.com/news/articles/2016-10-20/saudi-arabia-to-select-*

Saudi Arabia is not the only Muslim state to be pursuing a nuclear future. Turkey also announced an ambitious "peaceful" atomic power program shortly after Iran's nuclear enrichment efforts were revealed in 2002 and expressed an interest in 2008 in enriching its own uranium.[148] Given Turkish qualms about Iran acquiring nuclear weapons, the possibility of Ankara developing a nuclear weapons option (as it previously toyed with doing in the late 1970s)[149] must be taken seriously. In addition, Algeria and Egypt (political rivals) and Syria (a historical ally of Iran) all have either attempted to develop nuclear weapons options or refused to forswear making nuclear fuel, a process that can bring them within weeks of acquiring a bomb. Algeria now has enough plutonium and the skills to separate it from spent fuel to make several bombs' worth.[150] Egypt, which has long complained about Israeli nuclear weapons and previously attempted to get nuclear weapons, just announced its intention to tender bids

---

*nuclear-power-plant-site-very-soon.*

148. See "Turkey Considers Uranium Enrichment for Own Nuclear Power Plants," *RIA Novosti*, January 15, 2008, available from *http://en.ria.ru/world/20080115/96832054.html* and "Japan's Energy Pact with Turkey Raises Nuclear Weapons Concerns," *Asahi Shimbun*, January 7, 2014, available from *http://ajw.asahi.com/article/behind_news/politics/AJ201401070060*.

149. Turkish nuclear engineers in the late 1970s were asked by their government to investigate how plutonium from spent light water reactor fuel might be used to make nuclear explosives. They determined that it was quite feasible. Cf. Hans Rühle, "Is Turkey Secretly Working on Nuclear Weapons?" *The National Interest*, September 22, 2015, available from *http://nationalinterest.org/feature/turkey-secretly-working-nuclear-weapons-13898* and U.S. Department of Energy, Office of Nonproliferation and International Security, "International Safeguards: Challenges and Opportunities for the 21st Century," NNSA report NA-24, National Nuclear Security Administration, Washington, DC, October 2007, pp. 93-94.

150. See Bruno Tertrais, "Alternative Proliferation Futures for North Africa," in *The Next Arms Race*, pp. 205-38, available from *http://npolicy.org/books/Next_Arms_Race/Ch7_Tertrais.pdf*.

for its first, large power reactor.[151] Israel, meanwhile, continues to make nuclear weapons materials at Dimona,[152] and all of these states have nuclear-capable missile systems (see Figure 14 below):

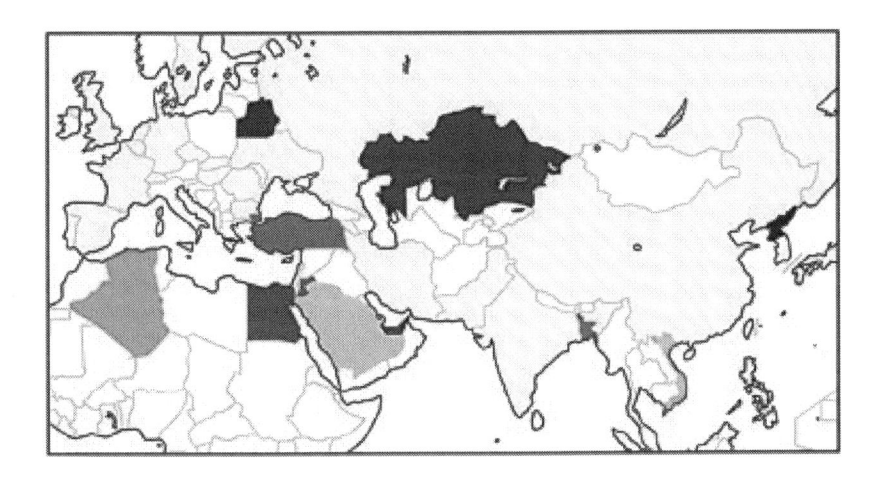

*Note: States in beige already have established nuclear power programs.*

**Figure 14. States Planning to Have Their First Nuclear Power Reactor by or before 2035.**

Very little of this rhymes with the world a half century ago. In the early 1960s, the only countries with civilian nuclear power reactors were the United States, the UK, and Russia. The number now is 31 states. Most of these are in Eastern and Western Europe but, as the map above makes clear, other states in far less stable regions are

---

151. See "Egypt to Launch Global Tender for Nuclear Power Plant by End of 2014," *Ahram Online,* July 19, 2014, available from *http://english.ahram. org.eg/NewsContent/3/12/106618/Business/Economy/Egypt-to-launch-global-tender-for-nuclear-power-pl.aspx*; Rafael Ofek, "Egypt's Nuclear Dreams," *IsraelDefense,* February 11, 2013, available from *http://www.israeldefense.co.il/ en/content/egypts-nuclear-dreams*; and Shaul Shay, "Will Egypt Go Nuclear?" *Arutz Sheva,* September 13, 2012, available from *http://www.israelnationalnews. com/Articles/Article.aspx/12181*.

152. See Avner Cohen, "Paying Too Much for Insurance," *Haaretz,* June 6, 2014, available from *http://www.haaretz.com/opinion/1.597240*.

hoping to bring their first nuclear power plants online before 2035. This trend, particularly in the Far and Middle East, has strategic implications.

As already noted, each of these plants—even the most proliferation-resistant light water reactor types—can be regarded as a "nuclear bomb starter kit." Although the nuclear industry has consistently promoted the mistaken idea that the plutonium power reactors produce is unsuitable to make bombs, these reactors can be operated not only to produce large amounts of reactor-grade plutonium that can be made into bombs, but of weapons-grade and near-weapons-grade plutonium as well.[153] In fact, in their first 12-18 months of normal power production operation, these reactors can produce roughly 50 bombs' worth of near-weapons-grade plutonium. If refueled every 10 months, they can produce roughly 30 bombs' worth of weapons-grade plutonium.[154] Also, the plants can and have been

---

153. This point has long been understood in the nuclear weapons engineering community. See note 120. Thus, the Reagan administration formally proposed acquiring an unfinished Washington Power Supply System light water reactor in Washington State in 1987 to increase U.S. production of weapons plutonium and tritium. See Milton Hoenig, "Energy Department Blurs the Line Between Civilian, Military Reactors," *Bulletin of the Atomic Scientists* 43, no. 5, June 1987, pp. 25-27, available from *http://books.google.com/books?id=pQYAAAAAMBAJ &pg=PA25&dq=wppss+weapons+plutonium+production+doe&hl=en&sa=X &ei=yISkU7mvB9froAS5_YKoCQ&ved=0CCQQ6AEwAQ#v=onepage&q=wp pss%20weapons%20plutonium%20production%20doe&f=false* and *Oversight Hearing on Potential Conversion of WPPSS 1 Commercial Nuclear Power plant to a Production Reactor, Before the House Subcommittee on General Oversight and Investigations of the Committee on Interior and Insular Affairs,* Hearing held in Portland, OR, 100th Cong., First Session (1988), Ser. No. 100-42, Washington, DC: GPO, 1988, available from *http://babel.hathitrust.org/cgi/pt?id=pst.000014 315848;view=1up;seq=1.*

154. Lawrence Livermore National Laboratory and Stanford University's Center for International Security and Cooperation determined that a standard one-gigawatt electrical light water reactor of the sort the United States pledged to North Korea as part of the 1994 Agreed Framework (which is similar to the light water reactor at Bushehr, Iran) would produce 300 kilograms of "fuel-grade" plutonium,

used as covers to acquire weapons related technology, hardware and training.[155] Finally, the massive amounts of low-enriched fresh fuel stored at these reactors for safety reasons can afford a source of enriched uranium to jump start a uranium enrichment weapons option.[156] That's why efforts are made to control the export of these plants and why they are routinely inspected to guard against military diversions.[157]

---

which is nearly weapons-grade in the first 12 to 18 months of operation and the rector could be operated to continue to produce 150 kilograms of "essentially" weapons-grade plutonium every 9 to 10 months. See Michael May, et al., "Verifying the Agreed Framework," report CGSR-2001-001, Center for Global Security Research, Lawrence Livermore National Laboratory, Livermore, CA, April 2001, p. 65, available from *http://iis-db.stanford.edu/pubs/12020/ VAF-June.pdf.* On the weapons utility of this "beginning of life" fuel-grade plutonium as compared to weapons- and super weapons-grade plutonium, see the analysis of former weapons designer Harmon Hubbard in Victor Gilinsky, et al., *A Fresh Examination of the Proliferation Dangers of Light Water Reactors*, Nonproliferation Policy Education Center, Arlington, VA, October 22, 2004, available from *http://www.npolicy.org/article_file/A_Fresh_Examination_of_ the_Proliferation_Resistance_of_Light_Water_Reactors.pdf.*

155. See Susan Voss, "Scoping Intangible Proliferation Related to Peaceful Nuclear Programs: Tracking Nuclear Proliferation within a Commercial Nuclear Power Program," in Henry Sokolski, ed., *Moving Beyond Pretense: Nuclear Power and Nonproliferation*, Carlisle, PA: Strategic Studies Institute, 2014, pp. 149-183, available from *http://www.npolicy.org/books/Moving_Beyond_Pretense/Ch6_Voss.pdf.*

156. See Gilinsky, et al., *A Fresh Examination of the Proliferation Dangers of Light Water Reactors.*

157. On the less than comprehensive character of these inspections and diversion worries this raises, see "Nuclear Safeguards: In Pursuit of the Undoable: Troubling Flaws in the World's Nuclear Safeguards," *The Economist,* August 23, 2007, available from *http://www.economist.com/node/9687869* and Henry Sokolski, "Assessing the IAEA's Ability to Verify the NPT," in *Falling Behind: International Scrutiny of the Peaceful Atom*, pp. 3-61 available from *http:// npolicy.org/thebook.php?bid=5#intro.*

As for declared nuclear fuel making plants—uranium hexafluoride and enrichment facilities, plutonium separation and fuel fabrication plants, etc.—there is a deeper problem that relates to the limits of International Atomic Energy Agency (IAEA) safeguards themselves. Even under ideal circumstances, the Agency allows that with commercial-sized plants, it can lose track of special nuclear material. The margins of statistical error associated with the inspection of these plants are egregiously large. Consider the reprocessing plant Japan wants to operate at Rokkasho. In this case, the agency can be expected to lose track of roughly 250 kilograms (i.e., roughly 50 first-generation bombs' worth) a year. Another way to put this is that nearly 50 bombs' worth of weapons-usable plutonium could possibly go missing from Rokkasho without setting off any international inspection alarms at all.[158]

Will the world be able to cope with the further spread of such "peaceful" nuclear facilities? Given the additional noted missile, fissile, and weapons trends, what, if anything, can be done to avoid their military diversions or worse—more widespread nuclear weapons competitions and, far worse, a possible accidental or intentional use of nuclear weapons?

---

158. See Marvin M. Miller, "Are IAEA Safeguards on Plutonium Bulk-Handling Facilities Effective?" reprinted in *Nuclear Power and the Spread of Nuclear Weapons*, Paul Leventhal et al., eds., Washington, DC: Brassey's, 2002, p. 273.

# WHAT MIGHT HELP

These trends invite disorder. How much depends on how well the United States, Russia, China, and other key states deal with them.

Despite its strained relations with Moscow over Ukraine, the United States is still committed to negotiating more nuclear weapons reductions with Russia.[159] New START is supposed to be followed eventually by an agreement that will cover both strategic and theater nuclear arms in Europe. The Obama administration was committed to bringing the CTBT into force, and is on record trying to secure an international agreement to end the production of fissile material for nuclear weapons. The United States has encouraged all countries to protect civilian and military nuclear facilities and stores of weapons-usable nuclear materials against theft or

---

159. See, e.g., Department of State, "Press Availability for G7," Remarks of John Kerry, Secretary of State, Hiroshima, Japan, April 11, 2016, available from *https://web.archive.org/web/20170114005426/https://www.state.gov/secretary/remarks/2016/04/255689.htm*; Office of the Press Secretary, "Statement by National Security Advisor Susan E. Rice on the Five-Year Anniversary of the New START Treaty Entry into Force," February 5, 2016, available from *https://obamawhitehouse.archives.gov/the-press-office/2016/02/05/statement-national-security-advisor-susan-e-rice-five-year-anniversary*; and Guy Faulconbridge and William James, "Trump's offer to Russia: an end to sanctions for nuclear arms cut - London Times."

sabotage. And the U.S. has tried to persuade nonweapons states to forgo reprocessing or enrichment to make their own nuclear fuels.

But these U.S. nuclear control initiatives, even if successful, still leave much to be done. Several related areas cry out for greater attention: nuclear and missile developments in China and East Asia, the global spread of "peaceful" nuclear technology, and the continued failure to develop a consistent, broad approach to preventing nuclear proliferation. This suggests three recommendations.

**1. Clarify China's strategic military capabilities and promote nonproliferation and arms control measures that limit strategic weapons in Asia.** Most current nuclear arms control agreements (e.g., the Limited Test Ban Treaty, the CTBT, FMCT, limits on missile defenses, SALT, START and INF) were originally designed to limit arms competitions between the United States and Russia. The NPT was initially designed to reduce the prospects of nuclear proliferation mostly in Europe. As the world's economic and strategic center of gravity shifts toward Asia, though, it would make sense to tailor more of our control efforts toward this region.

*Wither Beijing?*

This means, first of all, clarifying China's strategic capabilities. Beijing's revelations that it has built 3,000 miles of deep tunnels, to protect and hide its dual-capable missiles and related nuclear warhead systems, suggest the need to reassess estimates of China's nuclear-capable missile and nuclear weapons holdings and plans. Are Beijing's revelations disinformation designed to intimidate? Or is it hiding more military assets than we currently assess it has? What is it planning to acquire and deploy? How much military fissile material—plutonium and highly-enriched uranium—does China currently have on hand? How likely is it that China has or will militarize or expand its fissile material holdings? How might China militarize its civilian nuclear infrastructure? How many different types of nuclear weapons does it have or intend to deploy? How much fissile material does each type require? How many missile reloads does China currently have; how many is it planning to acquire? How extensive are Chinese deployments of multiple warheads for the country's missiles and how much further might China expand these deployments? For which missile types and in what numbers? How many nuclear and advanced conventional warheads is China deploying on its missiles, bombers, submarines, and artillery? What are its plans for using these forces? How might these plans relate to China's emerging space, missile defense, and anti-satellite capabilities? All of these questions, and more, deserve review within the U.S. government, with America's allies, and, to the extent possible, in cooperation with India, Russia, and China as well.

As a part of this review, it also would be helpful to game alternative war and military crisis scenarios that feature China's possible use of these forces. These games should be conducted at senior political levels in American and allied governments. Conducting such games should also inform U.S. and allied arms control policies and military planning. With regard to the latter, a key focus would have to be how one might defend, deter, and limit the damage that Chinese nuclear and nonnuclear missile systems might otherwise inflict against the United States, its bases in the Western Pacific, America's friends and allies, and Russia.

This could entail not only the further development and deployment of active missile defenses, but of better passive defenses (e.g., base hardening and improving the capacity to restore operations at bases after attacks; hardened command, control, and communication systems; etc.) and possibly new offensive forces—more capable, long-range conventional strike systems to help neutralize possible offensive Chinese operations.

Yet another focus for such gaming would be to clarify the likely consequences of Japanese or South Korean acquisition of nuclear weapons. These games should be held routinely, bilaterally and multilaterally with our allies and friends and, at times, with all of the key states, including China, represented by informed experts and officials. The aim of such games would not only be to understand just how risky Japanese and South Korean nuclear proliferation might be, but to clarify the risks China and North Korea will run if they continue to build up their missile and nuclear forces.

*Controlling Nuclear Missiles*

Such gaming should also encourage a review of Washington's current arms control agenda. Here several specific ideas, which are particularly relevant to Asia, deserve attention. First among these is talks with China, Russia, and other states about limiting ground-based, dual-capable ballistic and cruise missiles. China possesses more of these systems than any other state. Counting American, Russian, Indian, Pakistani, North Korea, South Korean, and Chinese ground based missiles, Asia is targeted by more such missiles than any other region.

Unlike air and sea-based missiles, ground-launched systems can be securely communicated with and fired instantly upon command. As such, they are ideal for use in a first strike. These accurate, dual-capable missiles also can inflict strategic harm against major bases and naval operations when carrying conventional warheads.

Ronald Reagan referred to these weapons as "nuclear missiles," and looked forward to their eventual elimination. Toward this end, he concluded the INF Treaty agreement, which eliminated an entire class of ground-based nuclear-capable missiles, and negotiated the Missile Technology Control Regime (MTCR), which was designed to block the further proliferation of nuclear-capable missiles (i.e., rockets and unmanned air-breathing systems capable of lifting over 500 kilograms for a distance of at least 300 kilometers). With the promotion of space-based missile defenses, Reagan hoped to eliminate enough of such ground-based missiles to eliminate credible nuclear first strike threats.[160]

Which states have an incentive to eliminate these missiles? The United States eliminated all of its intermediate ground-launched missiles under the INF Treaty. Most of America's shorter-range missiles are either air-launched or below MTCR range-payload limits. As for U.S. ground-based ICBMs, they are all based in fixed silos. To avoid being knocked out in any major future nuclear exchange, these missiles may have to be launched on warning. Russia, on the other hand, has a large, road-mobile ICBM force. At the same time, it is worried about growing numbers of long-range, precision missiles that both the United States and China are developing that it cannot easily defend against.[161]

India and Pakistan have ground-launched ballistic missiles, but some of their most seasoned military experts have called for the elimination of short-range missiles, arguing that these weapons are only likely to escalate border disputes.[162] As for China, it has

---

160. See Martin Anderson and Annelise Anderson, *Reagan's Secret War: The Untold Story of His Fight to Save the World from Nuclear Disaster,* New York: Three Rivers Press, 2009.

161. See, e.g., Kipp; note 100; and "US Concerned by China's New Hypersonic Missile," *The Voice of Russia,* January 29, 2014, available from http://sputniknews.com/voiceofrussia/news/2014_01_29/US-concerned-by-Chinas-new-hypersonic-missile-1459/.

162. See, e.g., RN Ganesh, "Nuclear Missile-Related Risks in South Asia," *The Next Arms Race,* pp. 305-56, available from http://npolicy.org/books/Next_Arms_Race/Ch10_Ganesh.pdf; Feroz Hassan Khan, "Prospects for Indian and Pakistani Arms Control," *The Next Arms Race,* pp. 357-86, available from http://npolicy.org/books/Next_Arms_Race/Ch11_Khan.pdf; and David Sanger, "U.S. Exploring Deal to Limit Pakistan's Nuclear Arsenal," *The New York*

much to gain by deploying more ground-launched missiles, unless, of course, such deployment causes India, Russia, and the United States to react militarily. The United States has been developing hypersonic boost glide systems that could provide it with prompt global strike options. It could base these systems either in the continental United States or in forward bases in the Western Pacific.[163] It also has hundreds of silo-based ICBMs that it could convert to deliver advanced nonnuclear payloads, including hypersonic boost glide systems.[164] Provoking the development of such U.S. weapons would not be in China's interest, or Russia's. Talks about reducing long-range, nuclear-capable ground-based missile systems and preventing the further spread of advanced missile technologies (e.g., hypersonic boost glide technology) to other states should be explored.[165]

---

*Times*, October 15, 2015, available from *http://www.nytimes.com/2015/10/16/world/asia/us-exploring-deal-to-limit-pakistans-nuclear-arsenal.html?_r=0*.

163. See Tim Walton, "Why We Need the Advanced Hypersonic Boost Weapon," *War on the Rocks* (blog), June 9, 2014, available from *http://warontherocks.com/2014/06/why-we-need-advanced-hypersonic-weapon/*.

164. Neither of these options would violate the INF Treaty, which does not cover hypersonic boost glide intercontinental systems. See Bill Gertz, "Inside the Ring: Pentagon goes hypersonic with long-range rapid attack weapon," *Washington Times*, March 19, 2014, available from *http://www.washingtontimes.com/news/2014/mar/19/inside-the-ring-pentagon-goes-hypersonic-with-long/?page=all*. Other options that have been discussed would. See, e.g., Barry D. Watts, *Long-Range Strike: Imperatives, Urgency and Options,* Washington DC: Center for Strategic and Budgetary Assessments, April 2005, pp. 62-68, available from *http://www.bits.de/NRANEU/docs/R.20050406.LRPS.pdf*.

165. For a fuller discussion, see the description of a RAND project led by Richard Speier titled "Hypersonic Missile Nonproliferation: Hindering the Spread of Hypersonic Glide Vehicles and Hypersonic Cruise Missiles," in Carl Robichaud, "New Technologies and the Nuclear Threat," *Carnegie Corporation of New York*, October 28, 2015, available from *https://www.carnegie.org/news/articles/new-age-nuclear-vulnerability/*. See also Richard H. Speier, K. Scott McMahon, and George Nacouzi, *Penaid Nonproliferation: Hindering the Spread of Countermeasures Against Ballistic Missile Defenses*, Santa Monica, CA: RAND

*Limiting Forward Nuclear Deployments*

Another arms restriction that should be considered is keeping the world's nuclear-armed states from deploying any additional nuclear weapons in peacetime on the soil of states that lack such weapons. An immediate concern is Saudi Arabia, which has been rumored to be interested in buying nuclear weapons either from China or Pakistan, or in getting either nation to deploy several of their warheads there. Under the NPT, it is permissible for nuclear weapons states to deploy their weapons in states that lack such weapons so long as these weapons stay under the "control" of the donor nuclear weapons state. This provision in the NPT was crafted in the 1960s to allow the United States to continue to deploy tactical nuclear weapons to NATO countries and East Asia, and for the Soviet Union to do so in Warsaw Pact countries.

Although the United States continues to forward base some of its weapons in Europe, long-range bombers and missile systems have made it possible to remove all of the forward deployed U.S. tactical nuclear systems from East Asia. Given that Washington is unlikely to reintroduce them or to increase existing deployments, it may be possible to broker some understanding to forbid any further deployments in exchange for Chinese and Pakistani pledges not to deploy any of their nuclear arms beyond their soil.

---

Corporation, 2014, available from *http://www.rand.org/pubs/research_reports/ RR378.html#recommendations* and Henry Sokolski, "Missiles for Peace," *Armed Forces Journal*, July 2010, available from *http://www.npolicy.org/article_file/ Missiles_for_peace-With_strong_conventional_strike_options_the_US_can_ lessen_nuclear_threats.pdf*. Also listen to the audio of a panel discussion, "Missiles for Peace," held at the Carnegie Endowment for International Peace in Washington, DC, September 13, 2010, available from *https://d2tjk9wifu2pr3. cloudfront.net/2010-09-13-Sokolski.mp3*. Also see Rachel Oswald, "Russian Expert Urges Multilateral Ban on Ground-Based Strategic Missiles," *Global Security Newswire*, February 13, 2014, available from *http://www.nti.org/gsn/ article/russian-expert-advises-getting-rid-icbms-encourage-multilateral-armscontrol/?utm_source=dlvr.it&utm_medium=twitter*.

With the turmoil in the Persian Gulf region, brokering such an understanding would be timely. It also would have the immediate advantage of engaging Pakistan, a non-NPT member, in some form of nuclear arms restraint. This is something that should be encouraged more generally with nuclear weapons-armed non-NPT members. Pakistan recently announced its willingness to forgo nuclear testing unilaterally.[166] Given Pakistan's rivalry with India, perhaps New Delhi could be persuaded to consider adopting such limits as well. Beyond this, other limits, including on nuclear fissile production might be sought, not only by Pakistan and India, but Israel. In this manner, one could begin to view states that are now outside the NPT as being instead potential NPT members in noncompliance—i.e., as states, which by taking steps toward nuclear restraint, might improve their current noncompliant NPT status. Additional nuclear restraints ought also to be promoted among the nuclear weapons armed states. Although, there is no clear legally binding obligation for the nuclear-armed states to disarm, the NPT encourages all states to make good faith efforts to do so.[167]

---

166. "Have declared unilateral moratorium on nuclear testing: Pakistan," The Indian Express, December 16, 2016, available from *http://indianexpress.com/article/world/have-declared-unilateral-moratorium-on-nuclear-testing-pakistan-4430382/*.

167. On the hortatory (vice legally binding) character of the NPT Article VI call for disarmament, see Christopher A. Ford, "Debating Disarmament: Interpreting Article VI of the Treaty on the Non-proliferation of Nuclear Weapons," *Nonproliferation Review* 14, No. 3, November 2007, pp. 401-28, available from *http://cns.miis.edu/npr/pdfs/143ford.pdf* and Cf. Gilinsky and Sokolski, "Serious Rules for Nuclear Power without Proliferation," in Henry Sokolski, ed., *Moving Beyond Pretense: Nuclear Power and Nonproliferation*, pp. 479-81, available from *http://www.npolicy.org/books/Moving_Beyond_Pretense/Ch16_SeriousRules.pdf*.

## Fissile Limits, Starting with China

If the United States could get other states to reduce their nuclear weapons capabilities in a verifiable fashion, it should be open to continuing to do so. Reaching new treaty agreements, though, ought not to be the only measure of progress. Although it may not be possible to conclude a fissile material cutoff treaty anytime soon, all of the other permanent members of the United Nations Security Council should press China to follow their lead in unilaterally forswearing making fissile material for weapons. This, in turn, could be helpful in pressing for moratoriums on "peaceful" nuclear fuel making of uneconomical nuclear weapons-usable fuels as well.[168]

In this regard, an informal pause on the commercial production, stockpiling, and recycling of plutonium would make sense. A good place to begin would be in East Asia and the Pacific, starting with China, the United States, Japan, and South Korea.[169] Here, it is worth noting that the 2012 report of the U.S. Blue Ribbon Commission on America's Nuclear Future determined that dry cask storage would make more economic sense for the United States to pursue in the management of waste and economic production of nuclear electricity than commercial plutonium recycling in the near and mid-term.[170] Meanwhile, America's efforts to convert weapons plutonium into commercial mixed oxide fuel (MOX) have

---

168. For the latest discussion of need to reduce states' production and stockpiles of civilian and military nuclear weapons-usable fuels, see Harold A. Feiveson, et al., *Unmaking the Bomb*, pp. 172-183.

169. See Brad Sherman, Jeff Fortenberry, and Adam Schiff, "Letter to President Obama Regarding the Production of Fissile Material in East Asia," June 10, 2016, available from *http://www.npolicy.org/article.php?aid=1317&rtid=4*.

170. See Blue Ribbon Commission on America's Nuclear Future, *Report to the Secretary of Energy*, Washington, DC: Blue Ribbon Commission on America's Nuclear Future, January 2012, pp. xii, xiv, 30, 98, 112, 118, available from *energy.gov/sites/prod/files/2013/04/f0/brc_finalreport_jan2012.pdf*.

encountered financial and technical difficulties.[171] As for Japan's planned plutonium reprocessing and fast reactor programs, Tokyo will have trouble implementing them given its reduced reliance on nuclear power and its termination of its only demonstration sized breeder at Monju. South Korea wants to recycle plutonium in a prototype integrated fast reactor, but this program may well get pushed back considerably. Also, its planned first fuel loading will be low-enriched uranium, not plutonium-based fuel.[172]

China is working with AREVA to build a commercial reprocessing plant nearly identical to the Rokkasho plant in Japan. A sticking point, though, is siting. So far, Beijing has been unable to select a site its public can humor. According to nuclear analysts, Beijing might build this large commercial reprocessing plant by 2030, have it separate plutonium for 10 to 20 years, and stockpile this material to fuel a fleet of commercial breeder reactors.[173] This view, in turn, is

---

171. See Steve Mufson, "Obama Plan to de-fund Savanah River Plutonium Conversion Plant Draws Fire," *The Washington Post*, February 25, 2016 available from *https://www.washingtonpost.com/business/economy/obama-plan-to-de-fund-savannah-river-plutonium-conversion-plant-draws-fire/2016/02/25/71428a72-db6e-11e5-925f-1d10062cc82d_story.html*.

172. See "Japan official calls for scrapping of troubled Monju reactor," *CBC News*, September 20, 2016, available from *http://www.cbc.ca/beta/news/technology/japan-monju-reactor-1.3770197* and Ferenc Dalnoki-Veress, Miles Pomper, Stephanie Lieggi, Charles McCombie, and Neil Chapman, *The Bigger Picture: Rethinking Spent Fuel Management in South Korea*, Occasional Paper no. 16, Monterey, CA: Center for the Nonproliferation Studies, 2013, pp. 23-25, 37-50, available from *http://cns.miis.edu/opapers/pdfs/130301_korean_alternatives_report.pdf*.

173. On the Chinese protests against the possible construction of this plant at Lianyungang, a city in Jiangsu Province, see, e.g., Chris Buckley, "Thousands in Eastern Chinese City Protest Nuclear Waste Project," *The New York Times*, August 8, 2016, available from *http://www.nytimes.com/2016/08/09/world/asia/china-nuclear-waste-protest-lianyungang.html* and Brian Spegele, "China Looks to Placate Nuclear-Project Protesters," The Wall Street Journal, August 10, 2016, available from *http://www.wsj.com/articles/china-cracks-down-on-nuclear-*

driven by the expectation that uranium yellowcake will be unavailable after 2050 for anything less than $130 (current) per pound (i.e., 300 percent more than the price today).[174]

This uranium price projection is speculative and rebuttable. What isn't is the potential military utility of China's civilian plutonium program. As already noted, the commercial-sized reprocessing plant the Chinese nuclear establishment may decide to build could produce enough plutonium for roughly 1,500 first-generation bombs annually. Assuming China's first breeder reactor came online by 2040, its first fueling with plutonium would come only after China had amassed well over 15,000 weapons' worth of plutonium.

Of course, if any of the three East Asian states begins to reprocess plutonium commercially, the other two would almost certainly follow, as much as a security hedge against each other as for any civilian purpose. At a minimum, the United States, France, and Russia should refrain from promoting large fast reactors in the region.[175] For similar reasons, China, Japan, and South Korea are

---

*project-protests-1470734568*. The 2030 date was recently confirmed by The World Nuclear Association. See "Nuclear growth revealed in China's new Five-Year Plan," *World Nuclear News*, March 23, 2016, available from *http://www.world-nuclear-news.org/NP-Nuclear-plans-revealed-in-Chinas-new-Five-Year-Plan-2303166.html*.

174. See, e.g., Zhongmao Gu, "Envision of Nuclear Energy Development in China," April 2014, presentation at the Nonproliferation Policy Education Center Alternative East Asian Nuclear Futures conference held February 25-27, 2014 in Honolulu, Hawaii, available from *http://npolicy.org/article.php?aid=1257&rid=2*.

175. On this last point, see Henry Sokolski, "How France is Fueling Japan and China's Nuclear 'Race'" *The National Interest*, November 6, 2015, available from *http://nationalinterest.org/feature/how-france-fueling-japan-china%E2%80%99s-nuclear-race-14271* and Sokolski, "Can East Asia Avoid a Nuclear Explosive Materials Arms Race?"

each interested in significantly expanding their capacity to enrich uranium even though there is a surfeit of uranium enrichment capacity world-wide. To head this off, it would be helpful to call for a freeze on the deployment of any additional commercial uranium enrichment capacity in China, Japan, and South Korea (and North Korea, if possible).[176]

As already noted, the United States and Russia maintain surplus nuclear weapons and nuclear weapons materials stockpiles, and India, Israel, Pakistan, China, Japan, France, and the UK hold significant amounts of nuclear explosive plutonium and uranium. This fissile material overhang increases security uncertainties as to how many nuclear weapons these states might have or could fashion relatively quickly. Given the verification difficulties with the proposed fissile material cutoff treaty and the improbabilities of such a treaty being brought into force, it would be useful to consider control alternatives.[177]

One idea, backed by several analysts and former officials, is a voluntary initiative known as the fissile material control initiative (FMCI).[178] It would call on nuclear weapons-usable material pro-

---

176. See Frank Von Hippel, Civilian Nuclear Fuel Cycles in Northeast Asia, paper presented the Panel on Peace and Security of North East Asia, Nagasaki, Japan, November 20, 2016, available from *http://npolicy.org/article_file/Civilian%20Nuclear%20Fuel%20Cycles%20in%20NE%20Asia%2028Oct2016%20%28rev.%202%29.pdf*.

177. See Christopher A. Ford, "Five Plus Three" and "Preparing for 2010."

178. For the earliest presentation of this concept, see Brian G. Chow, Richard H. Speier, and Gregory S. Jones, *A Concept for Strategic Material Accelerated Removal Talks (SMART)* DRU-1338-DoE, RAND Corporation, Santa Monica, CA, April 1996, available from *http://www.rand.org/content/dam/rand/pubs/drafts/2008/DRU1338.pdf*. Also see Robert J. Einhorn, "Controlling Fissile Materials and Ending Nuclear Testing," presented at an international conference on nuclear disarmament, "Achieving the Vision of a World Free of Nuclear Weapons," held in Oslo, Norway, February 26-27, 2008, available from *http://*

ducing states to set aside whatever fissile materials they have in excess of their immediate military or civilian requirements for either final disposition or internationally verified safekeeping. Russia and the United States have already agreed to dispose of 34 tons of weapons-grade plutonium, and have blended down 683 tons of weapons-grade uranium for use in civilian reactors. Much more could be done to dispose of and end production of such weapons-usable nuclear materials, not only in the United States and Russia, but also in other fissile-producing states, including those in Asia.[179]

**2. Encourage nuclear supplier states to condition their further export of civilian nuclear plants upon the recipients forswearing reprocessing spent reactor fuel and enriching uranium and press the IAEA to be more candid about what it can safeguard.** Will Iran's pursuit of "peaceful" nuclear energy serve as a model for Saudi Arabia (which says it wants to build 16 large power reactors before 2035), Turkey (which says it plans to build 20), Egypt (1), and Algeria (3)? When asked, none of these countries' officials have been willing to forgo making nuclear fuel. So far, only Turkey and the UAE have ratified the IAEA's tougher nuclear inspection regime under the Additional Protocol. There also is the outstanding

---

*www.ctbto.org/fileadmin/user_upload/pdf/External_Reports/paper-einhorn.pdf.*

179. It should also be noted that although China's and South Korea's fast reactor and plutonium recycling plans are ambitious, they are not yet locked in. China's fast reactor program is not yet fully funded. There is money to build pilot facilities, but not enough to operate them year-round. Nor, as already noted, has the Chinese government yet identified a specific construction site for its planned large commercial sized reprocessing plant. As for South Korea's program, it is still a matter caught up in the implementation of the U.S.-South Korean civilian nuclear cooperative agreement. See International Panel on Fissile Materials, *Plutonium Separation in Nuclear Power Programs*, pp. 19-29, 73-79; Chris Buckley, "Chinese City Backs Down on Proposed Nuclear Fuel Plant after Protests," *The New York Times*, August 10, 2016, available from *http://www.nytimes.com/2016/08/11/world/asia/china-nuclear-fuel-lianyungang.html?_r=0*; and note 131.

issue of whether the United States will eventually authorize South Korea to recycle U.S.-origin nuclear materials.

All of this should be a worry, since, as already noted, the IAEA cannot find covert enrichment or reprocessing facilities or reactor plants with much confidence (cf. recent history regarding nuclear plants in Iran, Iraq, North Korea, and Syria). Once a large reactor operates in a country, fresh low-enriched uranium becomes available and raises the possibility that it could be seized for possible further enrichment to weapons-grade in a covert or declared enrichment plant. Alternatively, the reactor's plutonium-laden spent fuel could be reprocessed to produce many bombs' worth of plutonium. Unfortunately, IAEA inspections at declared, commercial-sized uranium hexafluoride and enrichment plants, plutonium separation facilities, and plutonium fuel production plants could lose track of several scores of bombs' worth of nuclear explosive material annually.

*The Gold Standard*

Given these points and recognizing that the authority to inspect anywhere at any time without notice is not yet available to the IAEA (even when it operates under the Additional Protocol), any state's pledge not to conduct reprocessing or enrichment could not be fully verified in a timely manner. Still, securing such a legal pledge would have some value: It would put a violating country on the wrong side of international law if and when it was found out, and would make such action sanctionable. This may not be as much as one wants or needs, but it is far more of a deterrent to nuclear misbehavior than what current nonproliferation limits afford.

Other than the United States, no nuclear supplier state (i.e., Russia, France, Japan, China, or South Korea) has yet required any of its prospective customers to commit to not enrich uranium or reprocess spent fuel to extract plutonium, or to ratify the Additional Protocol.

Worse, the United States itself has backed away from insisting on these conditions (often labeled the nonproliferation "Gold Standard" for U.S. civilian nuclear cooperation).[180]

There is some support in the U.S. Congress for making it more difficult to finalize any future U.S. nuclear cooperative agreements with nonnuclear weapons states like Saudi Arabia unless they agree to the U.S.-UAE nuclear cooperative conditions.[181] These congressmen believe that by taking the lead on imposing such nonproliferation conditions, the United States would be in a much better position to persuade other nuclear supplier states to do the same.

---

180. See Victor Gilinsky, "'Flexible' Nuclear Trade," *National Review Online*, February 10, 2014, available from *http://www.nationalreview.com/article/370671/flexible-nuclear-trade-victor-gilinsky*; Henry Sokolski, "Putting Security First: The Case for Amending the Atomic Energy Act," prepared testimony for the Senate Foreign Relations Committee hearing on "Section 123: Civilian Nuclear Cooperation Agreements," January 30, 2014, available from *http://www.npolicy.org/article.php?aid=1244&rtid=8*; and "Obama's Nuclear Mistake: The President Converts Bush's Anti-Proliferation 'Gold Standard' into Lead," *National Review Online,* February 7, 2012, available from *http://www.nationalreview.com/article/290330/obamas-nuclear-mistake-henry-sokolski*.

181. See Elaine M. Grossman, "U.S. Senate Panel Backs Vietnam Nuclear Trade Pact, But Tightens Conditions," *Global Security Newswire,* July 23, 2014, available from *http://www.nti.org/gsn/article/us-senate-panel-backs-vietnam-nuclear-trade-pact-tightens-conditions/* and "Bipartisan Bill Filed to Heighten Oversight of U.S. Nuclear Trade," *Global Security Newswire,* December 13, 2013, available from *http://www.nti.org/gsn/article/bipartisan-bill-filed-heighten-oversight-us-nuclear-trade/*. Also see H.R. 3766, "A Bill to Amend the Atomic Energy Act of 1954 to Require Congressional Approval of Agreements for Peaceful Nuclear Cooperation with Foreign Countries, and for Other Purposes," introduced in the 113th Congress on December 12, 2013, available from *https://www.govtrack.us/congress/bills/113/hr3766/text*; H.R. 1280, "A Bill to Amend the Atomic Energy Act of 1954 to Require Congressional Approval of Agreements for Peaceful Nuclear Cooperation with Foreign Countries and Other Purposes," introduced in the 112th Congress on March 31, 2011, available from *https://www.govtrack.us/congress/bills/112/hr1280*; and "Chairman Ros-Lehtinen Opening Statement: HR1280, The Atomic Energy Act of 1954," April 20, 2011, available from *http://www.youtube.com/watch?v=Qrvz2_gzik8*.

With the Japanese and South Koreans, close U.S. nuclear cooperation and security guarantees could be leveraged to secure these countries' agreement to such conditions on their nuclear exports. They and the Chinese want to export reactors based on U.S. designs. It is unclear whether they can do so legally to states that do not have a nuclear cooperative agreement with the United States. China, meanwhile, needs all the help it can get from the United States to complete the Westinghouse-designed reactors it is building and the Chinese variant it is pegging much of its nuclear future on. As for France, it may have difficulty exporting reactors without significant Asian support.[182] With Russia as well as China, the United States should be more candid about the safety issues construction and operation of their reactors present and offer to renew or expand nuclear cooperation to help resolve these concerns in exchange for upgrading the nonproliferation conditions on these countries' nuclear exports.[183] Each of these points constitutes nuclear leverage that

---

182. See Energy Collective, "AREVA Struggles to Dig Out of Debt," March 25, 2015, available from *http://www.theenergycollective.com/dan-yurman/2208496/areva-struggles-dig-out-debt*; John Lichfield, "UK Nuclear Strategy Faces Meltdown As Faults Are Found in Identical French Project," *The Independent*, April 18, 2015, available from *http://www.independent.co.uk/news/uk/home-news/uk-nuclear-strategy-faces-meltdown-as-faults-are-found-in-identical-french-project-10186163.html*; Stephen Chen, "French Warnings on Nuclear Reactors Being Built in China's Guangdong," *South China Morning Post*, April 15, 2015, available from *http://www.scmp.com/news/china/article/1762861/french-warning-nuclear-reactors-being-built-guangdong*; ASN, "Flamanville EPR Reactor Vessel Manufacturing Anomalies," Press Statement, July 4, 2015, available from *http://www.french-nuclear-safety.fr/Information/News-releases/Flamanville-EPR-reactor-vessel-manufacturing-anomalies*; "Japan's JNFL in Talks on Taking Areva Minority Stake: Source," *Reuters*, December 13, 2016, available from *http://www.reuters.com/article/us-areva-restructuring-idUSKBN14227K*; and "Japan's JNFL in Talks on Taking Areva Minority Stake: Source," *Reuters*, December 13, 2016, available from *http://www.reuters.com/article/us-areva-restructuring-idUSKBN14227K*.

183. The United States suspended all civilian nuclear cooperation with Russia shortly after it invaded the Crimea. On the questionable safety of Russian and Chinese reactor construction, see Tara Patel and Benjamin Hass, "China Regulators

Washington could exploit to push broader supplier application of gold standard nonproliferation requirements with each of the nuclear supplier states.[184]

*Timely Detection*

It also would be helpful if the IAEA was more honest about what kinds of nuclear activities and material holdings it can actually safeguard effectively—i.e., which ones it can inspect so as to detect military diversions in a timely fashion and which ones it cannot. As it is, the IAEA is unwilling to make public its assessments of the Agency's ability to meet its own timeliness detection goals (which are hardly strict). Meanwhile, no state, including the United States, has yet done such an assessment of the Agency's safeguards effectiveness.[185]

---

'Overwhelmed' As Reactor Building Steams Ahead," *Bloomberg News,* June 20, 2014, available from *http://westhawaiitoday.com/news/nation-world-news/china-regulators-overwhelmed-reactor-building-steams-ahead*; "Concerns over China's Nuclear Power Expansion," *Chinadialogue*, April 24, 2014, available at *https://www.chinadialogue.net/blog/6932-Concerns-over-China-s-nuclear-power-expansion/en*; Christina MacPherson, "China's Nuclear Safety Prospects Are Not Good," *nuclear-news*, October 29, 2013, available from *http://nuclear-news.net/2013/10/29/chinas-nuclear-safety-prospects-are-not-good/*; Eve Conant, "Russia's Nuclear Reactors Could Take Over the World, Safe or Not," *Scientific American,* October 2013, available from *http://www.scientificamerican.com/article/russias-nuclear-reactors-could-take-over-the-world-safe-or-not/*; and Quamrul Haider, "How Safe Are the Russian Civilian Nuclear Reactors?" *Daily Star* (Lebanon)*,* June 12, 2013, available from *http://archive.thedailystar.net/beta2/news/how-safe-are-the-russian-civilian-nuclear-reactors/*.

184. See Emily B. Landau and Shimon Stein, "To Prevent Another Iran Disaster, Fix Nuclear Enforcement," *The National Interest,* June 8, 2016, available from *http://nationalinterest.org/feature/prevent-another-iran-disaster-fix-nuclear-enforcement-16516*.

185. See *World At Risk: The Report of the Commission on the Prevention of WMD Proliferation and Terrorism*, Washington, DC, December 2, 2008, pp. 49-50, available from *http://www.cfr.org/terrorism/world-risk-report-commission-*

In the 1960s, 70s, 80s, and 90s, when only a handful of states lacking nuclear weapons were interested in enriching uranium or separating plutonium from spent reactor fuel, this lax approach may have been tolerable. Today, however, Japan, South Korea, Argentina, Brazil, South Africa, Egypt, Turkey, Saudi Arabia, Iran, Vietnam, and Jordan are all either making enriched uranium, reprocessing spent reactor fuels, or reserving their "right" to do so. All of these states are members of the NPT and have pledged not to acquire nuclear weapons. Should we assume that none of them will ever cheat? What confidence should we have that the IAEA would be able to detect possible diversions early enough for the other NPT members to intervene to prevent them from producing nuclear weapons?

Currently, the IAEA's own nuclear safeguards guidelines set routine inspection intervals to approximate the time the Agency estimates it is needed to convert certain special nuclear materials into bomb cores. The IAEA's ability to verify production figures at large uranium hexafluoride; reprocessing, uranium enrichment, and plutonium and mixed oxide fuel fabrication plants though, is limited. Not only does the Agency have difficulty detecting abrupt diversions in a timely fashion (i.e., it may only be able to learn of diversions after they have occurred), but the margins of error associated with the IAEA's ability to detect small, incremental diversions are equivalent to many bombs' worth every year. In either case, once a state has enough fissile material to make a bomb, it could break out well before the IAEA or other states could intervene to prevent nuclear weapons from being built.

These facts are troubling. What makes them doubly so is that the IAEA has yet to share these specifics publicly in any detail. Worse, it continues to claim that it can safeguard these materials and plants (i.e., provide "timely detection" of possible military nuclear diversions of), when, in fact, in many cases, it cannot.

*prevention-wmd-proliferation-terrorism/p17910.*

It is essential that inspectors and diplomats distinguish between what inspectors can merely monitor (i.e., inspect to provide confidence that major diversions have not taken place sometime in the past) from what they can actually safeguard (i.e., inspect to assure detection of military diversions early enough so outside parties have sufficient time to block actual bomb making). If this distinction were made clear, governments could fully appreciate and, hopefully, restrict, nuclear activities and holdings that are unsafeguardable and hence dangerous.[186] This, in turn, would make promoting tougher nonproliferation standards, like the Gold Standard, much easier.

**3. Anticipate and ward off nuclear proliferation developments before recognized redlines have been clearly violated.** One of the regrettable legacies of the Cold War is the habit U.S. and allied government officials have acquired of waiting for irrefutable evidence of undesirable, foreign nuclear weapons developments before taking action. This must change.

After the Soviet Union first acquired nuclear weapons in 1949, the West's aim in competing against Russia was not so much to prevent it from acquiring more strategic weapons as it was to prevent it from gaining strategic superiority. For this purpose, it was sufficient that Western military forces remained more modern and sufficiently numerous to deter Soviet offensive capabilities—i.e., that Russia's strategic technology stayed roughly one or more generations behind ours so that its strategic deployments could never

---

186. See note 156; Victor Gilinsky and Henry Sokolski, "Is the IAEA's Safeguard Strategic Plan Sufficient?" a paper presented at the International Atomic Energy Agency Symposium on International Safeguards: Linking Strategy, Implementation and People, October 22, 2014, Vienna, Austria, available from *http://npolicy.org/article_file/IAEA_Safeguard_Strategic_Plan.pdf*; and Trevor Finlay, *Proliferation Alert! The IAEA and Noncompliance Reporting,* Report no. 2015-04, Cambridge, MA: Project on Managing the Atom, October 2015, available from *http://belfercenter.ksg.harvard.edu/files/proliferationalert-web.pdf.*

change the relative balance of power. If Russia deployed a new strategic nuclear rocket, Washington would focus on what the Soviets had built and built a bigger or better U.S. version, developed some new passive or active defenses or built counter offensive forces that could neutralize the new Soviet weapon system.

After the United States and Russia ratified a number of strategic arms limitation agreements, any Russian strategic nuclear deployment that exceeded agreed limits became a matter for diplomatic adjudication. In either case, U.S. or allied action turned on detecting and verifying the violation of agreed or implicit redlines. Fortunately, in this competition, the Soviets ultimately failed to keep up with the United States and its allies. Moscow's failed attempts to do so only helped bankrupt it financially and politically.[187]

*Competitive Strategies*

That was the Cold War. In our current efforts to prevent horizontal proliferation, the objective is quite different. Instead of merely trying to stay ahead of a proliferating state militarily, our aim must be to prevent it from acquiring certain weapons altogether. Being able to detect states' possible violations of pledges not to acquire these weapons is necessary.

The problem is that verifying such detections is much more awkward than detecting and verifying Soviet strategic weapons developments. Whereas detecting Soviet arms developments was often deemed to be an intelligence success and frequently prompted

---

187. On these points, see Octavian Manea, "Lessons from Previous Competitive Strategies," *Small Wars Journal*, July 6, 2014, available from *http://smallwarsjournal.com/jrnl/art/lessons-from-previous-competitive-strategies* and "The Art of Tailoring Competitive Strategies," *Small Wars Journal*, March 24, 2014, available from *http://smallwarsjournal.com/jrnl/art/the-art-of-tailoring-competitive-strategies*.

policy or military actions, detecting nuclear proliferation today is bad news—it only confirms that our nuclear nonproliferation policies have failed. Also, more often than not, by the time one verifies a nonproliferation violation, it is too late to roll it back unless one takes relatively extreme diplomatic or military measures. It is not surprising, then, that in more than a few proliferation cases—e.g., with Israel, Pakistan, North Korea, South Africa, and India—U.S. officials often averted their gaze from, denied, or downplayed intelligence that these states had acquired or tested nuclear weapons.[188]

In some cases, though, the United States and its allies succeeded in preventing nuclear proliferation. The most prominent cases included getting Taiwan, South Korea, South Africa, Argentina, Brazil, Ukraine, and Libya to give up their nuclear weapons programs. In these cases, the United States and its allies had a long-term regimen of nonproliferation sanctions and export controls in place well before the state in question ever acquired nuclear weapons (e.g., in the cases of Libya and South Africa), or acted well before there was clear proof that nuclear weapons were in hand or were going to be retained (e.g., with Taiwan, South Africa, South Korea, and Ukraine).[189]

---

188. See Victor Gilinsky, "Sometime Major Violations of Nuclear Security Get Ignored," in Henry Sokolski, ed., *Nuclear Materials Gone Missing: What Does History Teach?* Arlington, VA: The Nonproliferation Policy Education Center, 2014, available from http://www.npolicy.org/books/Materials_Unaccounted_For/Ch4_Gilinsky.pdf; Robert Zarate, "The Nonuse and Abuse of Nuclear Proliferation Intelligence in the Cases of North Korea and Iran," and Leonard Weiss, "The 1979 South Atlantic Flash: The Case for an Israeli Nuclear Test," in Henry Sokolski, ed., *Moving Beyond Pretense: Nuclear Power and Nonproliferation,* Carlisle, PA: Strategic Studies Institute, 2014, pp. 345-71, 373-409, available from http://www.npolicy.org/books/Moving_Beyond_Pretense/Ch14_Zarate.pdf and http://www.npolicy.org/books/Moving_Beyond_Pretense/Ch13_Weiss.pdf.

189. See Mitchell Reiss, *Bridled Ambition: Why Countries Constrain Their Nuclear Capabilities,* Washington, DC: Woodrow Wilson Press, 1995, pp. 90-129 and Eugene Kogan, "Coercing Allies: Why Friends Abandon Nuclear

What these and other less well known nonproliferation successes suggest is the desirability of creating long-term, country-specific strategies that initially eschew dramatic actions. These strategies could be developed along several lines. In the case of Libya and South Africa, the West relied heavily on long-term, bureaucratically institutionalized economic sanctions and export controls as well as a vigilant proliferation intelligence watch on each country's nuclear weapons-related programs and timely political interventions.

An even more aggressive approach would create a set of tailored competitive strategies that would work backwards from nuclear futures U.S. officials wanted to avoid towards futures they thought were better. The aim here would be to set a series of mid-term (i.e., 10-20 year) goals that would drive and guide our diplomatic, economic, military, and intelligence efforts to shape more peaceful futures.[190] Rather than wait to act until there is proof of a nuclear weapons program, officials would act earlier, taking modest steps to ward off incipient nuclear weapons programs or to support positive policies that might reduce the targeted state's interest in initiating such programs in the first place.[191]

---

Plans," paper presented at the American Political Science Association Annual Meeting, Chicago, IL, August 2013, available from *http://live.belfercenter.org/files/kogan-apsa-aug-2013.pdf*.

190. See David J. Andre, "Competitive Strategies: An Approach against Proliferation" and Henry D. Sokolski, "Nonproliferation: Strategies for Winning, Losing, and Coping," in Henry D. Sokolski, ed., *Prevailing in a Well-Armed World: Devising Competitive Strategies against Weapons Proliferation,* Carlisle, PA: Strategic Studies Institute, 2000, pp. 3-25, 51-64, available from *http://npolicy.org/books/Well-Armed_World/Ch3_Sokolski.pdf*. Also see Henry D. Sokolski, "Fighting Proliferation with Intelligence," *ORBIS* 38, no. 2, Spring 1994, pp. 245-60, available from *http://fas.org/irp/threat/fp/b19ch16.htm*.

191. For specific examples, see note 189 and Henry Sokolski, "Ending South Africa's Rocket Program: A Nonproliferation Success," Nonproliferation Policy Education Center, Arlington, VA, August 31, 1993, available from *http://www.npolicy.org/article.php?aid=458&tid=2*.

## What Might Help

*Hard-headed Internationalism*

An integral part of working such competitive strategies would be a willingness to promote the kinds of nonproliferation and arms control proposals noted above. This would require a hard-headed kind of internationalism. In the 1960s and 1970s, when U.S. and allied arms control policies were premised upon finite deterrence—i.e., on the evils of targeting weapons and defending against them, and on the practical advantages of holding innocents at risk in the world's major cities—arms control rightly became an object of derision by serious security planners.[192] Since then, it almost has become an article of conservative, Republican faith that arms con-

---

192. Although today there are virtually no respectable, hawkish or hard-headed works on what sorts of nuclear arms control might be useful; this was not always the case. Thirty or more years ago, before arms control practice became dominated by mutual assured destruction theorizing, several distinguished military scientists including Fred Ikle, Albert Wohlstetter, Leon Sloss, Donald Brennan, and Alain C. Enthoven all believed unconstrained nuclear competitions and strategic weapons proliferation was less than optimal and seriously considered what sort of arms control might be practical. See, e.g., Albert and Roberta Wohlstetter, "On Arms Control: What We Should Look for in an Arms Agreement," unpublished draft essay, May 20, 1985, available at the Hoover Institution Archive, Albert and Roberta Wohlstetter Papers, Notes, Box 118, Folder 16, available in Robert Zarate and Henry Sokolski, eds., *Nuclear Heuristics: Selected Writings of Albert and Roberta Wohlstetter,* Carlisle, PA: Strategic Studies Institute, 2009, pp. 472-500, also available from *http://www. npolicy.org/userfiles/file/Nuclear%20Heuristics-On%20Arms%20Control.pdf*; Albert Wohlstetter and Brian C. Chow, "Arms Control that Could Work," *Wall Street Journal,* July 17, 1985, available from *http://www.npolicy.org/article_file/ Arms_Control_That_Could_Work.pdf*; Fred Charles Iklé, "Nth Countries and Disarmament," *Bulletin of the Atomic Scientists* 16, no. 10, December 1960, pp. 391-94, available from *http://www.tandfonline.com/doi/abs/10.1080/00963 402.1960.11454156?journalCode=rbul20#.V2BWToSDGko*; Leon Sloss and M. Scott Davis, eds., *Game for High Stakes: Lessons Learned in Negotiating with the Soviets,* New York: Harper Business, 1986; Alain C. Enthoven and K. Wayne Smith, *How Much Is Enough: Shaping the Defense Program, 1961-1969,* New York: Harper and Rowe Publishers, Inc., 1971; and Donald G. Brennan, ed., *Arms Control, Disarmament and National Security,* New York: George Braziller, 1969.

trol is self-defeating. Most liberal Democrats, on the other hand, believe that it deserves unquestioned support.[193]

Any serious effort to reduce future nuclear threats will need to move beyond this ideological divide. Certainly, any nuclear threat reduction effort that supports U.S. and allied aims will be difficult to sustain unless it complements some larger diplomatic effort. The best way to start would be to put our Cold War fascination with mutual assured destruction theorizing aside and focus instead on what is most likely to reduce the chances of war, nuclear proliferation, and nuclear weapons use.[194]

International law also has become increasingly stylized to restrain states from taking military action. Its practical impact, however, has been to restrain those states least likely to take such action even when such action is called for. As a result, international law has lost its standing among many of those most concerned about the safety and security of their country. To be sure, there are limits to what any international legal structure can achieve without the backing of sovereign military power.[195] But in the past, international law and the promotion of justifiable sovereign power were seen as being mutu-

---

193. Cf., J. Peter Scoblic, *US vs. Them: Conservatism in the Age of Nuclear Terror,* New York: Penguin Books, 2009 and John Wohlstetter, "Nuclear Zero 2012: We Disarm While Others Arm," *Human Events,* September 12, 2012, available from *http://humanevents.com/2012/09/12/nuclear-zero-2012-we-disarm-while-others-arm/.*

194. See Henry D. Sokolski, "Preface," in Henry D. Sokolski, ed., *Getting MAD,* pp. v-vi, available from *http://npolicy.org/books/Getting_MAD/Preface_Sokolski.pdf* and Idem., "Taking Proliferation Seriously," *Policy Review.*

195. See Henry R. Nau, "Conservative Internationalism: A Smarter Kind of Engagement in World Affairs,"National Review Online, August 2, 2014, available from *https://www.nationalreview.com/nrd/articles/358318/conservative-internationalism* and Conservative Internationalism: Armed Diplomacy under Jefferson, Polk, Truman, and Reagan, Princeton, NJ: Princeton University Press, 2013.

ally supportive. We need to get back to this earlier understanding. Like maintaining peace, this is neither hopeless nor automatic.[196]

In any effort to return to this view, the given suggestions are a reasonable place to begin. It is clearly desirable to reduce the number of nuclear weapons, the amount of nuclear weapons-usable materials, the number of plants that make them, the number of long-range nuclear-capable missiles, and the number of states possessing these nuclear assets. It may be imprudent to make such cuts unilaterally or without effective verification, but we should be clear about our willingness to compete militarily and diplomatically to realize such reductions in a manner that avoids such risks. Indeed, on this last point, there should be no hesitation. Less, in this case, *would* be better.

## *Thinking Ahead*

Recently, a friend and former senior official under three presidents (both Republican and Democratic) quipped that with most nuclear weapons proliferation problems, officials initially are loath to act because they believe there is no clear problem, and then, when they

---

196. Since George F. Kennan's publication of American Diplomacy, Chicago: University of Chicago, 1984, there has been a popular belief that international law that claims to promote international security is generally at odds with our national security. However, there are alternative views that could and have guided U.S. diplomacy and national security policies. Principal among these is the life work of Elihu Root, U.S. Secretary of State under President Theodore Roosevelt, Secretary of War from 1899 to 1904, Nobel Peace Prize winner, founding architect of the Permanent Court of International Justice, and founder of the American Society of International Law. On his career and advocacy of promoting international laws to promote and protect America's national interests, see Erik A. Moore, "Imperial International Law: Elihu Root and the Legalist Approach to American Empire," Essays in History, 2013, available from *http://www.essaysinhistory.com/articles/2013/172* and Robert E. Hannigan, *The New World Power: American Foreign Policy, 1898-1917*, Philadelphia: University of Pennsylvania Press, 2002.

finally are convinced that the problem is real, they insist there is no solution. This is a pathology for inaction. It also is unnecessary. In fact, some of the toughest nuclear proliferation problems can be neutralized well before they are fully realized, and, in key cases, have been.

From 2013 through 2015, I held a series of workshops on alternative nuclear futures in East Asia. These meetings, which included Chinese, Korean, Japanese, U.S., and Russian security and energy experts and officials, focused on how each country would react if they or their neighbors either acquired nuclear weapons or ramped up the number of nuclear arms they already had. First, I was warned that no one would attend. Then, I was told that if they did come, no one would speak. Finally, I was advised, if they spoke, they would not get along. All of these predictions proved to be mistaken. Instead, there were candid Chinese and Korean exchanges about Japan's stockpiling of plutonium and Japanese and Russian anxieties expressed about the opacity of China's nuclear weapons program. There was a problem, though: All of the participants, including government officials from each state (including the United States), confided in me that the discussions we were having could never be conducted by or within each of their respective governments—the topics simply were too sensitive.

This is bad enough. Yet, the challenge of working difficult security issues (including nuclear weapons proliferation) runs even deeper. Operating outside of government, one has the freedom not only to be vocal, but consistent (two things that are difficult to do while in office). Yet, exercising this freedom often draws criticism from those in or close to power as being dangerously radical or impractical. There is no easy response to this. One strong possibility, however, is that too many government officials are failing to do their jobs while too few analysts outside government are pointing this out. There is, after all, a strong temptation (particularly among officials who are ambitious or eager to please) to avoid issues that, if mishandled, could result in catastrophe (either for themselves or for others). Those outside of government, who wish to maintain and expand their network of contacts, share such caution.

Giving in to this temptation, however, risks backing into and compounding our most serious, avoidable problems. Thus, the nuclear crisis in Iran was made worse by more than 20 years of inattention and consistent down playing of the risks Iran's program posed. When U.S. officials finally began to focus in the early 2000s on the Iranian nuclear threat, Iran's nuclear program had become so mature and intractable that the available responses were limited either to acts of war or diplomatic backsliding. Not surprisingly, this only encouraged an unhealthy political polarization over the issue.[197]

With nuclear weapons proliferation, these pitfalls can be avoided, but only if those in and outside of government focus on proliferation problems earlier and more seriously than they have to date. Of course, some will protest that we can ill afford to concentrate on anything but the most pressing nuclear crises—whether it be North Korea, Iran, or our relations with Moscow. "Solving" these matters, it's argued, is imperative to avoid immediate and certain nuclear disaster and, therefore, to assure nuclear restraint and peace for the long haul. Perhaps. But any honest assessment would suggest that our most urgent problems no longer allow for any simple solutions. If so, our optimism and hopes would be better directed more toward futures we can shape now than on correcting present crises our past neglect has all but determined.

---

197. See Henry Sokolski, "Ten Regrets."

# INDEX

2nd Artillery Corp, 57

## A

Afghanistan, 18
Algeria, 55, 92, 109
America. *See* United States
AREVA, 106
Australia, 62

## B

Beijing, 71-72, 88, 98, 106
　　*See also* China
breeder reactor. *See* reactor
Broken Arrow, 21
Bushehr, 19, 36
　　*See also* Iran

## C

Cheney, Dick, 14, 32
Cheonan, 84
China, 3, 7, 17, 19, 29, 32-33, 37, 39, 42, 46, 50, 52, 53, 55, 57, 59, 60-62, 66-74, 79-83, 85-86, 88-90, 97-100, 102-103, 105-108, 110, 112, 122
Churchill, Winston, 55
Cold Start, 64
Cold War, 30, 32, 35, 39, 45, 55-56, 58, 88, 115-116, 120
competitive strategies, 116-119

Comprehensive Nuclear-Test-Ban Treaty (CTBT), 24-25, 97-98
Cuban Missile Crisis, 39

## D

DF-41, 70
Dimona, 19, 36-37, 93
　　*See also* Israel

## E

Egypt, 25, 37, 42, 62, 92, 109, 114
enrichment, 37, 53, 80-83, 89, 91-92, 95-97, 108, 110, 114, *See also* uranium

## F

fast reactor. *See* reactor
Fissile Material Cut-off Treaty (FMCT), 25-26, 98
France, 14, 17, 39, 45-48, 53-55, 57, 62, 74, 107-108, 110, 112
Fukushima, 74-76
　　*See also* Japan

## G

Gaulle, Charles de, 9
Gold Standard, 110-113, 115
Gulf War, 20

## H

hawk, 4, 5, 7, 10, 11-12, 14-15, 28-29, 32, 42, 73, 119
Hussein, Saddam, 20, 36
hypersonic boost glide systems, 102

## I

India, 17, 19, 25-26, 29, 32, 37, 39-40, 42, 45-46, 50, 52, 55, 57, 64-67, 72, 89-90, 99-102, 104, 108, 117
  New Delhi, 64, 90, 104
intercontinental ballistic missile (ICBM), 61, 70, 90, 101-102
Intermediate-Range Nuclear Forces Treaty (INF Treaty), 73, 100-102
International Atomic Energy Agency (IAEA), 14-15, 96, 109, 109-114
Iran, xi, 7, 11, 18-19, 24-26, 32, 34, 36-37, 40, 42, 51, 55, 61-62, 90-92, 109-110, 114, 123
  Tehran, 55
Iraq, 4, 19, 20, 36-37, 42, 55, 110
  Osirak, 19, 36
Islamabad, 90. *See also* Pakistan
Israel, 17, 19, 25, 29, 32, 37, 39, 40, 45-46, 51, 57, 61-62, 66, 92-93, 104, 108, 117
  Dimona, 19, 36-37, 93

## J

Japan, 3, 7, 10-11, 14-15, 18, 32, 34-35, 40, 49-50, 53, 55, 69, 72, 74-88, 96, 99, 105-114, 122
  Fukushima, 74-76
  Rokkasho, 76-79, 85, 96, 106
  Tokyo, 76, 82, 87-88, 106

## K

Kahuta, 37 *See also* Pakistan
Kennedy, John F., 24

## L

light water reactor, 74, 80, 92, 94
  *See also* reactor
Los Angeles, 69

## M

Minatom/Tenex, 80
  *See also* Russia
Missile Technology Control Regime (MTCR), 100-101
mixed oxide fuel (MOX), 105, 114
Moscow, 33, 37, 45, 65, 72-73, 97, 116, 123
  *See also* Russia
Mueller, John, 9-10, 14-15
multiple independently targetable re-entry vehicles (MIRVs), 70

# Index

## N

neorealist, 4, 8, 11, 14-15
New Delhi, 64, 90, 104
   *See also* India
New START, 24-25, 73, 97
no first use, 39, 57, 69
North Atlantic Treaty Organization (NATO), 10, 54, 61-62, 66, 91, 103
North Korea, 7, 11, 18, 24-26, 29, 32, 34, 37, 39-40, 42, 45-46, 51, 54-55, 57, 60, 79, 84-86, 88, 100, 108, 110, 117, 123
   Pyongyang, 29, 86, 88
Norway, 36
nuclear-capable missile, 45, 53, 61-62, 67, 70, 73, 93, 100, 121
   ballistic missile, 59-61, 69, 90, 101
   cruise missile, 84, 90, 100
Nuclear Nonproliferation Treaty (NPT), 2-3, 11, 14-15, 25-28, 42, 98, 103-104, 114
   three-pillars of, 3, 25-26
nuclear security summits, 24-25
nuclear terrorism, 7, 20-23, 29, 32, 35-36, 42

## O

Obama, Barack, 6, 24, 33, 97
Osirak, 19, 36
   See also Iraq

## P

Pakistan, 18-19, 25, 29, 37, 39, 42, 45, 46, 51, 57, 62, 64-66, 81, 90, 100-101, 103-104, 108, 117

Islamabad, 90
Kahuta, 37
plutonium, iv, 48-52, 68, 74-79, 84, 89-92, 94-96, 98, 105-110, 114, 122
   reactor-grade, 50, 76-78, 89, 94
   weapons-grade, 49-52, 76-77, 82-83, 89, 94-95, 109-110
Prague, 7, 25
Putin, Vladimir, 34
Pyongyang, 29, 86, 88
   *See also* North Korea

## R

reactor, 19, 36-37, 50, 74-83, 89-95, 106-114
   breeder, 106-107
   light water, 74, 80, 92, 94
   fast, 74, 106-107
Reagan, Ronald, 16, 94, 100, 101
recycle, 106, 110
reprocess, 50, 74, 84, 91, 96-97, 106-107, 109-110, 114
Rokkasho, 76-79, 85, 96, 106
   See also Japan
Romney, Mitt, 33
Rumsfeld, Donald, 14-15
Russia, v, 3, 6-7, 17, 21, 29, 32-39, 42, 45-62, 66-67, 70-74, 78-81, 88-89, 93, 97-102, 107-116, 122
   Minatom/Tenex, 80
   Moscow, 33, 37, 45, 65, 72-73, 97, 116, 123
   Soviet Union, 19, 32, 35, 37, 45, 49, 53, 88, 103, 115-117
   Yamantau, 59

## S

safeguards, 27, 89, 96, 109, 113-115
Saudi Arabia, 7, 18, 40, 55, 62, 90-92, 103, 109, 111, 114
Seoul, 83-84, 87-88
  *See also* South Korea
South Africa, 37, 114, 117-118
Zaafaraniyah, 37
South Korea, 3, 7, 11, 18, 32, 34, 40, 42, 51, 53, 55, 60-61, 79-80, 83-88, 99-100, 105-110, 112, 114, 117, 118
  Seoul, 83-84, 87-88
  Yeonpyeong Island, 84
Soviet Union. *See* Russia
spent fuel, 74-75, 84, 92, 109-110, 114
submarine-launched ballistic missile (SLBM), 14, 90
Syria, 26, 37, 42, 92, 110

## T

Taiwan, 42, 69, 72, 117-118
Tehran, 55. *See also* Iran
timely detection, 109-110
Tokyo, 76, 82, 87-88, 106
  *See also* Japan
Trump, Donald, 32, 73
Turkey, 7, 18, 40, 42, 55, 92, 109, 114

## U

Ukraine, 97, 117-118
United Arab Emirates (UAE), 40, 62, 109, 111
United Kingdom (UK), 14-15, 17, 45, 48, 53-57, 62, 87, 93, 108
United States (U.S.), 1-3, 6-8, 11-15, 17-22, 25, 29, 32-34, 37, 39, 42-62, 66-67, 69-76, 84-89, 93, 97, 105, 110, 112, 15-123
uranium, iv, 48, 51-53, 68, 76, 80-84, 89-92, 95-96, 98, 106-114
  enrichment, 37, 53, 80-83, 89, 91-92, 95-97, 108, 110, 114
  hexafluoride, 96, 110, 114
  highly-enriched (HEU), iv, 48, 52, 83
  low-enriched, 95, 110
  weapons-grade, 49-52, 76-77, 82-83, 89, 94-95, 109-110
URENCO, 80

## V

Vietnam, 18, 29, 39, 114

## W

Waltz, Kenneth, 8, 14-15
Warsaw Pact, 10, 103
Washington DC, 3, 24, 35, 45, 72-73, 83-88, 100, 103, 113, 116
  *See also* United States
weapons-usable, 21, 67, 75, 96-97, 105, 108, 121
Wohlstetter, Albert, 1, 119
Wohlstetter, Roberta, 1
World Nuclear Association, 80
World War (WWII, WWIII), 10, 19, 35-36

## Y

Yamantau, 59 *See also* Russia
Yeonpyeong Island, 84
    *See also* South Korea
Yesin, Viktor, 71

## Z

Zaafaraniyah, 37
    *See also* South Africa
zero nuclear weapons, 16-17, 28

Made in the USA
Middletown, DE
27 March 2017